Modern Writers

Douglas Gifford

Neil M. Gunn and
Lewis Grassic Gibbon

GUNN & GIBBON

Oliver & Boyd

Acknowledgements

The author and publishers are grateful to Curtis Brown Ltd., on behalf of the Estate of Lewis Grassic Gibbon for permission to quote from his work (all material copyright The Estate of Lewis Grassic Gibbon); and to Faber & Faber Ltd., for permission to quote from Gunn's *The Silver Darlings* and Mr Dairmid Gunn for permission to quote from other work by Neil Gunn.

Oliver & Boyd
Robert Stevenson House
1-3 Baxter's Place
Leith Walk
Edinburgh EH1 3BB
A Division of Longman Group Ltd

ISBN 0 05 003197 X Cased
*   0 05 003198 8 Paperback*

First published 1983

Printed by
Kyodo-Shing Loong Printing Industries Pte Ltd Singapore

Contents

When critics are cited in the text the reader is referred to the Bibliography for further details.

1 Introduction

A book of this size cannot do critical justice to Gunn's twenty and Gibbon's eleven novels, let alone their volumes of stories and other essays. In my opinion *The Silver Darlings* is far and away Gunn's finest novel, and arguably the finest balance of metaphysical speculation and concrete epic-making that any fiction-writer in English has achieved this century. Certainly for Gunn it is the point of fusion of the strands of his ideas and practice, with *Highland River* to me coming next as the work in which he tried to find a prose-poetry to express his unique version of Wordsworthian and natural epiphany. Similarly with Gibbon. I consider *A Scots Quair* and *Sunset Song* as his finest work, again showing the point of fusion of strands in the writer's practice. Next to this (and with a few of the short stories) I admire *Spartacus*, in many ways a finer expression of what *Grey Granite* was trying to say. Since these works are the most likely to be used and studied, I decided to devote two-thirds of this study to a consideration and implicit comparison of them. My study is thus as follows: the introduction; a chapter on Gunn, outlining biographical facts and tracing swiftly the development in the novels, concentrating on *Highland River*; chapter three on Gibbon, with the same pattern, ending in a discussion of the great Scottish short stories and a discussion of *Spartacus*; chapter four is given over entirely to *A Scots Quair*, thus following on from chapter three; while chapter five discusses (as the climax to the 'Scottish Renaissance') *The Silver Darlings*. A brief conclusion sums up the relationship of Gunn's and Gibbon's work, and their influence.

Gunn and Gibbon belong with novelists like Forster, Lawrence and Woolf, and poets like T. S. Eliot and Yeats, in their contribution to that great revival of spiritual awareness after the Great War which saw itself as struggling to find a way out of man's self-created wasteland of the mind. Eliot's *The Waste Land* (1922), that ritual

1

of self-purgation which called on archetypes and spiritual practice of many cultures through many ages to try to salvage a higher self in man, is fundamental to Gibbon and Gunn. I will argue that the Scottish Renaissance writer's wasteland had other roots than Eliot, but it is appropriate here to note that Eliot himself was only part of a creative consciousness in Europe brought about by loss of traditional faith after Darwin and Huxley's work. Sir James Frazer was the great Scottish anthropologist whose mammoth *The Golden Bough* (1890–1915) collected and classified ritual and myth over the world; Sigmund Freud, the psychoanalyst of the early twentieth century, enunciated the notion of our having a subconscious mind, more potent and mysterious in motivating our actions than hitherto dreamed; and Carl Jung, the 'heir apparent' to Freud who moved away from his master, liberated Freud's notions of the subconscious from Freud's narrowness of interpretation.

These men gave back spiritual hope to the modern writer, though Frazer would be surprised to know this since his collection of myth and ritual was presented as the material born of man ignorant and savage. But such material to Freud, as in *Totem and Taboo* (so influential on Gunn), was put to a different use from that its collector intended. Freud and Jung looked in the habits of primitive man for what they considered modern man to have overlooked. They discovered that the primitive mind functioned at levels more profound and relevant to us now than had been thought. Finn's relationship with the ancient ring of Druid stones called 'the House of Peace' in *The Silver Darlings* or Chris Guthrie's instinctive refuge at the Standing Stones of the Picts shapes their respect for primitive practices, finding in them a meaning which would not have been found by previous writers.

Thus we find E. M. Forster in *Howard's End* (1910) presenting civilised southern English families forced to recognise that they are not being true to something deep, instinctive and natural within themselves. They slowly regain sight of right 'ends' — thus the pun in the title — divesting themselves of social pretension and trusting rather the deeper rhythms of subconscious parts of their minds. And while much of this movement 'back to the land' went so far in the work of G. K. Chesterton, or Mary Webb, for example, as to move Stella Gibbons to satire in *Cold Comfort Farm* (1932), much of it moved into the mainstream of European literature. Lawrence's

The Rainbow (1915) shows man separated from his subconcious losing those instinctive urges which relate us to the animal world, to growing natural life, and to harmony — that rhythmic sense of 'one-ness' with the world around us glimpsed by Wordsworth and central to the modern novel of the post-war period, as in Virginia Woolf's *To the Lighthouse* (1925) and *Mrs Dalloway* (1927). Gunn and Woolf are particularly close here, in the notion of a 'moment of delight', when the essential goodness of life is made clear. In writers as far removed as Lawrence and Joyce one can see in the experiences of Ursula Brangwen of *The Rainbow* or Stephen Daedalus of *A Portrait of the Artist as a Young Man* (1916) a comparable use of 'epiphany'.

With the new respect given to the primitive came respect for legend and ritual. Jessie Weston's *From Ritual to Romance* (1920), an account of shared elements of religious mythology throughout world myth and religion, was one of the links between the anthropologists and the writer, giving to Eliot, Lawrence and Joyce 'the wasteland myth': the belief common to these writers and Gunn and Gibbon (as well as many of the Scottish writers like Muir and MacDiarmid and Soutar) that modern man has backed himself into a spiritual cul-de-sac or wasteland in which no spiritual refreshment is attainable, since God's existence has been eliminated by reason. Two images of wasteland are fused together: the modern, Kafka-esque image of a sordid and fragmented society, arid and unloving in non-community, and the image of myth, drawn from sources as diverse as Norse legend and Christian belief, in which the wasteland is the parched country, literally thirsting and fruitless, because it has offended its Gods. In the myth there recur the central figures who, by sacrifice or by being sacrificed, redeem the wasteland by propitiating the Gods. For our purposes all we must know is that the old kings of the Corn (and their sea counterparts, the Fisher kings) — and their queens — who are fruitless themselves, must die, and the new hero-king must emerge to save his people. It should be obvious immediately that Gunn and Gibbon make use of this idea in their epic novels, just as do Lawrence and Joyce. Thus Gunn and Gibbon are part of a European urge to find meaning behind society — in short, to rediscover God — in the mysterious recesses of our selves (our 'dark Gods' as Lawrence called them). These writers argue that it is in the mysteries of our consciousness and subconsciousness that the transcendental and spiritually important elements of our lives are to be found. Intuition, inspiration, instinct and dream are now of crucial importance, for in these processes we use what is holy and above the merely human in ourselves. Gunn and Gibbon are looking, above all else, for what Kurt Wittig called 'the source', God. What he says of Gunn is true of Gibbon and these other British writers; they are looking for:

> the pattern of life, the underlying ritual, the myth...in terms of man's ancestral past, in terms of the primordial ages before the dawn of history.

Finally it seems to me that in one way Gunn and Gibbon are descended from the central vision of English Romantic poetry. Gunn cited Wordsworth as central to his work, and Wordsworth's moment of timeless harmony, the Romantic vision of 'the other landscape' in *The Prelude*, the 'Ode on Intimations of Immortality' and 'Tintern Abbey', so often set in a natural world which actively prompts the vision, is basic to Gunn's vision. With Gibbon I speculate that it was the passionate, yearning Keats, hungry in the intuition of his own death for a stable vision of permanence (as in 'Bright Star' or 'Ode to a Grecian Urn') who can be seen in Gibbon's own poetry, and whose half-love for easeful death, despair at human agony, combined with an honesty which would not avoid the horror, still speaks in the darkest pages of Gibbon. To this extent Gunn and Gibbon are directly in the English Romantic tradition.

Whatever the external sources and influences, both Highland Gunn and Lowland Gibbon were aware of previous attempts in Scottish poetry and fiction to image the state of Scotland. What had the Scottish tradition to offer them?

No Scottish novelist till Gibbon deals seriously with the social and industrial changes which affected Scotland from the discovery of black band iron ore in the lowland coalfields in 1802. No novelist expresses the urbanisation which changed the face of Scotland more than any country in the world at the same period. What had Scottish fiction been doing instead?

4

Throughout the nineteenth century, Scottish fiction was either obsessed with the past, especially the Jacobite Rebellions and the covenanting times, or the dream of a rural 'neverland', a kailyard Eden. Two kinds of fiction were especially hateful to the twentieth-century Scottish writer. The first Edwin Muir called 'the escape to Scottland' (somewhat unfairly), and the second was the kailyard escape to the 'timeless village'. The first kind was of course encouraged by the example of Scott, and produced endless melodramas exploiting the bloody horrors of Scottish history as romance. Scott in novels like *The Antiquary* (1816) or *The Fair Maid of Perth* (1828), Stevenson in *The Black Arrow* (1888) and *St Ives* (1897), and writers from Margaret Oliphant to William Black, S. R. Crockett, Neil Munro and John Buchan all contributed to this. At best it had strong narrative, and at worst it became a cultural smoke-screen over the industrialised lowlands of Scotland. The 'kailyard' variety, although defended recently by Francis Hart as an Edenic vision and symbolic projection of a deep-down desire in Scots for a mythic green place, seems rather to me to be a deliberate tradition of falsification of social reality, condescension and exploitation. In the hands of John Wilson ('Christopher North', editor of *Blackwood's* magazine and Professor of Moral Philosophy at Edinburgh University from 1820), the kailyard novel became propaganda by the Tory establishment to drown the nineteenth-century movement in Scotland for political reform. In its successive writers' links with the Christian establishment of Victorian Britain (with William Robertson Nicoll and the *British Weekly*, 1886 on), and its prevalence as a genre among ministers and sons of the manse, from J. M. Barrie to Crockett and Ian Maclaren, its aim was hardly that of radical critique or creative unrest. Novels like Maclaren's *Beside the Bonnie Briar Bush* (1894) had painted the Scottish countryside as a place of pretty rural innocence, with peasants with hearts of gold, poor scholar-poets dying melodramatically in the arms of widowed mothers, attended by gruff church elders trying manfully to restrain their tears, with faithful collies and sunsets.

The House with the Green Shutters, and its 'successor', John MacDougall Hay's *Gillespie* (1914), paint a very different picture of Scottish country life. Instead of a pious peasantry, we find selfish, bigoted chauvinistic gossips who have lost charity and good-humour; and instead of the church lying at the heart of the community with its message of cheer, we find brutal and greedy small-town tyrants like John Gourlay the town carrier of the *House with the Green Shutters* and Gillespie Strang of MacDougall Hay's novel, the town merchant who drains the town's life-blood. Gunn remembered these novels when he wrote his first novel, *The Grey Coast*; and Gibbon *ends* part one of *Sunset Song* with the 'speak' summing up Kinraddie:

> So that was Kinraddie that bleak winter of nineteen eleven and the new minister, him they chose early next year, he was to say it was the Scots countryside itself, fathered between a kailyard and a bonny briar bush in the lee of a house with green shutters. And what he meant by that you could guess at yourself if you'd a mind for puzzles and dirt, there wasn't a house with green shutters in the whole of Kinraddie.

There was, however, a valid tradition of Scottish fiction, a 'school' of satiric examination of the 'state of Scotland' beneath these superficial images of Scotland.

This genuine tradition in fiction was brought into being by Walter Scott with that very different creative side of his personality which too rarely committed itself to the labour of transmitting his deepest and dark vision of Scotland. Scott's best fiction, in *Waverley* (1814), *Old Mortality* (1816), and *The Heart of Midlothian* (1818), attempted to show through symbolic pictures of history how Scotland had become a country divided in language and loyalties (Covenanters and Episcopalians, Jacobites and Hanoverians, Whigs and Tories) down to its essence. The themes of these novels are civil war, division within families, father against son, the 'divided country'. Scott rarely goes for the glorious periods of Scottish history, from Canmore to Alexander III, or the Wars of Independence to the Golden Age of James IV. Instead, he looks for the causes of that fatal division between Scotland's feelings for its past, its sentimental Jacobitism and its romantic love of its Rob Roys, and its prudent commercial eye to the future, its place in the Industrial Revolution, and its commonsense attitude to philosophy and economics which expresses itself in Adam Smith's pioneering work in political economy, *The Wealth of Nations* (1776).

Scott's heart backed the Highlanders and Prince Charles, the stern enthusiasm of the Moss troopers, Rob Roy, as symbols of that old Scotland he loved. His head realised sadly that Union with England had to be for the sake of commerce, for the future of the Baillie Nicol Jarvies of commercial Glasgow, and he thus set his romantic but doomed Highlanders and extremists of all kinds in a tragic and ironic fiction. To Scott, Scotland's destiny is to dream passionately but to fail tragically, the failure being brought about by opposing forces within Scotland itself. In appreciating Gibbon's and Gunn's creation of archetypal and regenerative figures like Chris Guthrie ('Chris Caledonia') and Finn of *The Silver Darlings*, we should not forget that Scott set the pattern for this kind of mythical figure of national regeneration. Such a one is Henry Morton in *Old Mortality*, and especially Jeannie Deans, who for the sake of mercy and the healing of vision 'takes on' the sick legal system, and in the end the monarchy of Britain itself. *The Heart of Midlothian* is Scott's attempt at symbolic regeneration, as *Kidnapped* and *Catriona* were, unsuccessfully, for Stevenson. His David Balfour epic was to show the need for integrity, charity and the quest for justice in a corrupt Scotland, and like Jeannie he too goes on a symbolic journey. It's a measure of the loss of hope in Stevenson by the end of the nineteenth century that David's quest ends in despair. 'Exile and cunning' is the lot of the serious Scottish fiction writer from Macdonald to Stevenson, Douglas Brown to Gibbon. Carlyle's departure, Hogg's withdrawal from central culture to his Border roots, Macdonald's disguised preaching on behalf of a religious consciousness utterly opposed to the Presbyterian, show that Scotland in the hundred years before Gunn and Gibbon was not welcoming to the artist who criticised it. Nevertheless, Hogg in the *Private Memoirs and Confessions of a Justified Sinner* (1824), Galt in *The Annals of the Parish* (1821), *Ringan Gilhaize* (1823), but especially in *The Provost* (1822) and *The Entail* (1823), Stevenson in *The Merry Men* (1882), the unfinished *Weir of Hermiston* (1896), in disguise in the English-set *Dr Jekyll and Mr Hyde* (1886), but especially in *The Master of Ballantrae* (1889) developed a line of trenchant satire on the Scottish personality which was to burgeon, with important results for Gibbon and Gunn, in *The House with the Green Shutters* (1901) by George Douglas Brown, and *Gillespie* (1914) by John MacDougall Hay.

These novels are preoccupied with disintegration of whole personality. They present families who are split to the point of murder, brother against brother, father against son, and finally self against self. The 'heart' and the 'head' are opposed; the feeling, oversensitive but repressed aspect of self and society are set against the unfeeling, excessive materialism and respectability. And Gunn's first novel, *The Grey Coast*, has Daun Tulloch, the brutal and prosperous farmer, directly descended from Brown's giant of materialism John Gourlay, and Hay's West Highland miser, Gillespie Strang. The concern of both with achieving final 'wholeness' and sense of complete self is latent in the Scottish tradition of 1814–1918.

This said, there is no doubt that in the nineteenth-century Scottish life and literature had stultified. The poetic inheritance of Burns, Scott and Hogg was stifling all but the occasional poem, such as Alexander Smith's 'Glasgow' (1857), a rare attempt to make poetry of the urban and industrial scene. There was a Scottish revival in the 1890s, led by Patrick Geddes, its vehicle the *Evergreen* magazine, its forms Celtic Twilight poetry and the short fiction of 'Fiona MacLeod' (William Sharp) and the Galloway idylls of Crockett. Such obvious imitation of the Irish revival was alien to the real roots of culture and politics in Scotland, and it was not until the full after-effects of the First World War were felt that a radical search for a valid Scottish tradition began. It was led by 'Hugh Mac-Diarmid' (Christopher Grieve) angered at having fought for the rights of small nations without knowing anything about his own.

MacDiarmid was not the be-all and end-all of the Renaissance. He denied this himself, pointing to the activity and achievement all around him. What is striking is the agreement amongst the Renaissance writers that 'what we are suffering from is an utter lack of tradition' (MacDiarmid in 1926); that there had occurred a crucial dissociation of sensibility in Scottish consciousness at the time of the Reformation (Muir, in *Scott and Scotland* (1932)) which had destroyed traditional wholeness of language and vision; that most images of Scotland offered by her creative writers in the last three hundred years had been untrue and debased; that the nature of the Celtic contribution to the Scottish tradition was not that which manifested itself in the 'Celtic Twilight' movement; and that instead of being a root-strength, the Scottish consciousness they inherited was debilitating. It is important here to see how 'tradition' was completely redefined within a short space of time, and to see that it was tradition that Gunn and Gibbon wanted to change, and re-embody, in the new Scottish cultural awareness.

The outstanding change is seen in the position which the Renaissance had clearly agreed to by 1934 (the year of completion of *A Scots Quair* and *Butcher's Broom*), in contrast to what the Scottish cultural consensus had been in 1800. Where the 'Scottish Enlightment' had broadly argued the need for improvement in manners, estates and city conditions, and for 'civilising' the barbaric Highlands, in developing the city-state as the right end of man's progress from primitive savagery, using orthodox religion to bolster this programme, and where the nineteenth-century fiction writers shared this view, the Renaissance writers denied this programme entirely. What programme did they put in its place?

The Scottish Renaissance is a remarkably unified and rewarding area, still astonishingly neglected inside and outside Scotland. With a rich variety of genres in Scots and English, the Renaissance is arguably the richest period of all Scottish literature. It arose around MacDiarmid and his 'Scots language' platform, but broadened to include Edwin Muir, Gunn, Eric Linklater, Gibbon, Naomi Mitchison, James Bridie and William Soutar. Many of these writers do not use Scots, and most are in no way subservient to the MacDiarmid dogmatic Scottish line. For example, Linklater's *Magnus Merriman* (1934) is a delightful picaresque satire on the entire Renaissance, with biting satire on MacDiarmid himself (as the poet Hugh Skene) at its heart. Muir and MacDiarmid were utterly opposed on the question of what languages the Rennaissance should use, Muir believing that Scots was dead for creative purposes. Against MacDiarmid's cultural nationalism, Gibbon was such an extremist that he would have welcomed a Chinese army of occupation and the abolition of 'Scottish' culture rather than put up with even a part of the Glasgow slums. There was a splendid divergence of opinion within the 'movement' — so much so that some have questioned whether such divergence permits the idea of a unified movement to survive. With hindsight, however, we can see beyond the Muir-MacDiarmid-Gibbon disagreements to the very strong core of agreement and shared ideals and symbols. A shared consciousness clearly underpinned the larger unity of the movement.

9

What are the main points of this 'shared consciousness'? First, a common attitude to the Scottish historical past. All the novelists — Gunn, Gibbon, Linklater, Mitchison, Fionn MacColla — agree that what occurred in the last thousand years of Scottish political and social history was mainly bad for Scotland; outstandingly so being the Scottish Reformation of 1560 and its consequences. (This view is shared by Muir, MacDiarmid and Soutar.) Add to this a broadly left-wing and Nationalist bias and a remarkable and sudden post-war revolution is clearly discernable in Scottish literature. If one considers what *The Silver Darlings* and *A Scots Quair* say about Scottish religion and social history, it will be obvious that there is running satire on the first in both and a common hatred of authoritarian and land-exploiting imperialist attitudes to traditional Community.

Secondly, there is the regenerative myth itself, loosely describable as a 'Golden Age' myth. This breaks company with the English movement in the fiction of Forster, Woolf, Lawrence and Joyce in that the Scots were aided by a sense of living tradition in legend and folklore stronger and deeper than their English contemporaries. The Scots suggest a clearer outline to their vision of the way back to the Lost Eden. 'Our river took a wrong turning somewhere, but we haven't forgotten the source,' says Gunn in *Highland River*. This statement represents the relationship which nearly all the protagonists of the major Scottish novels of the period have with their past. Using the concept of Jung's 'collective unconscious' (or Yeats' 'Great Memory'), characters like Chris Guthrie, Chae Strachan, even John Guthrie (in *A Scots Quair*) or Catrine McHamish, Roddie Sinclair and Finn McHamish (in *Silver Darlings*) are made by their authors to discover identity with their ancestors. The best introduction to how this is done is Gunn's opening to *Highland River* where the boy, Kenn, through the activity of catching the huge salmon, 'remembers' things about his atavistic self which he has never known or experienced in his short life. Stories told to him by his brothers of his ancestors, instincts bone-deep, a sense of myth, crowd in on him in a way which shows that he is perceiving the truths of an ancient way of life. There is, argue the Scottish writers, an inherent sense in modern man of a lost and better time, when direct appreciation of the basic relationships with Nature and Self was a better state of being than that

10

which has come about in our civilised society. This is the Golden Age consciousness. The writers vary in the degree to which they commit themselves to it. Gibbon and Gunn are extremely involved with such possibilities, while Muir and Soutar come somewhere between them and the more sceptical and qualified use of the myth by MacDiarmid and Linklater.

Further to myth, and at the root of why the Scottish writer is so strongly attracted to it, is the usage of local legend and folklore in all the work of the period, from poetry and drama to fiction. For the Scottish writer this is the essential warp and woof of his fabric. From Orkney to the Borders, the material survived social change and the Second World War in better shape than elsewhere. The major Scottish writers use the legends and quasi-historical figures and situations to establish a continuity between then and now — as in the drama of James Bridie, say, *The Anatomist* (1930) or *Mr Bolfry* (1943), or Soutar's ballad-based poetry like 'Birthday', or short stories like Linklater's 'The Goosegirl', 'Sealskin Trousers' or Mitchison's *Five Men and a Swan* (1958) or her ambitious novel on the theme of national unity, *The Bull Calves* (1947).

Lastly, there is a more subtle and complex use of dream and the supernatural. From the drunken and fantastic insights of MacDiarmid's *A Drunk Man Looks at the Thistle* to Chae Strachan's moonlight visions, from Muir's recollections of before the Flood to Finn's apprehension of the wise old Druid priest, the Scots writers present experience which transcends normal apprehension. This is the high point of their vision, when the modern Dead Self is seen to fall away and perception through what Gunn calls 'the fourth dimension' causes the perception of a better, ideal self. It is of course a surrogate religious experience, and MacDiarmid has attacked it as such — but it is, whether we accept it or not, the basis of *the art* of all these writers (even MacDiarmid himself) and especially the basis of the work of Gunn and Gibbon.

2 Neil Gunn's Highland River of Delight

The fundamental difference between the visions of Neil Gunn and Lewis Grassic Gibbon arises from the contrasting experiences of life for each. Gunn came from a harmonious community, loving and respecting his parents and forebears, whereas Gibbon hated his community and the effects that farming had on it. Gunn bonded himself with his beloved Highlands, finding in them rich poetic metaphor and a myth of regeneration, where Gibbon retreated from his north-east lowland crofting country to foreign parts and the Services and eventually a garden suburb town of London to write with a mixture of love and despair about what he saw as the death of traditional community.

When in 1956 Gunn came to write his autobiography, *The Atom of Delight*, he presented not so much a history of himself and his career as a metaphysical and deeply spiritual quest for Self. As such a quest obeys no rules of our factual world, so *The Atom of Delight* obeys none of the 'rules' of conventional autobiography. The external facts of Gunn's private and public life are secondary to an account of books he read which helped his quest or places which yielded moments of delight. From these, like Wordsworth in his 'emotion recollected in tranquility' and Proust re-searching for the essence of past significant experience, he distils the spirit or cracks the atom of delight.

Gunn came from Dunbeath, a small fishing and crofting village near Helmsdale. In contrast to Gibbon's land background, Gunn is land-and-sea orientated. The rhythms of life demanded that both be served at different periods in the year. For Gunn this memory of balance and harmony is elemental and life-enhancing, and all of his novels record the essential goodness of traditional community. Even in the gloomiest, like the *The Grey Coast* and *The Lost Glen*, the sense of a past wholeness is conveyed.

Critics have objected to what they think is Gunn's over-

12

sentimentalisation of Highland life, and to his emphasis on the 'spiritual superiority' of the Gael. They miss his point, and his reservations. Life was memorably and truly good in Gunn's communities, and Gunn tries to glean the essence of that goodness. He does not assert the superiority of the Gael, as numerous passages in his fiction from *The Lost Glen* to the pictures of the West coast in *The Silver Darlings* testify. Gunn knows that clearance, poverty, the effects of excessively Puritanical religion and progress have frequently debased or destroyed his race in many of its communities.

He was born on 8 November 1891, one of the youngest of a huge fishing and crofting family. The fishing was still busy, but about to die at the turn of the century, so that livelihoods would not be there for the boys. Three brothers emigrated to Canada; all died victims of the 1914–18 war. The memories of youth, as in *Morning Tide* and *Highland River*, although elegiac, are good, establishing in Gunn's mind the archetypal figures so strong in his fiction: the mother, centre of the house, enduring worry while the fishing took the men to sea in small boats for days, understandably wanting her sons to 'get on' and away from the cruel sea; the father, patriarchal and with a dignity gathered from his dangerous life, unobtrusive but powerful; the old man with accumulated memories and humorous wisdom; and, most of all, the boy, filled with wonder and about to be initiated into this simple but exciting world. Their music and story was rich, centuries old. The other diversion for boys and men was poaching — hardly a crime, to take fish or beast from the rivers and hills their forefathers had lived amongst for millennia, but fraught with danger from the watching gamekeepers of the absentee landlords who 'owned' these waters and moors. The watching keeper representing the danger of Authority in the outside world became a negative archetype in Gunn's fiction.

Gunn believes that the land *is* spiritual, animate and filled with living qualities. Like Gibbon's countryside, Gunn's *watches*. Kurt Wittig has noted the habit of the Scottish writer of making his land animate, with its living spirit. Gunn goes deeper than any in this process, for women partake of the Land, men of the Sea; Sutherland is 'beckoning, heedless, feminine' and Caithness 'simple, elemental, masculine'.

Gunn identifies all that can be found in spiritual search with what can be found in his home environment. Here is the answer to those who call him a 'local' or parochial novelist. Truth and discovery of self, as Ronnie tells Finn in *The Silver Darlings*, is to be found amongst one's own and in oneself. Travel and change of setting are irrelevant, unless they are found from a centre of truth. Universals are as likely to be found in a remote fishing village in Scotland's far north as in William Faulkner's deep south or Melville's American east coast.

The community of Gunn's childhood was moderate in religion, temperate in its fun and social manners, rich in texture — but the fullness and busyness passed. Gunn regretted the move from 'the independence of crofting and sea-fishing or any other natural industry to the dependence on tourism and sport', and chose the comparative independence of the Civil Service. He left his strath at 13 for two years in Galloway, then in 1906 went to London after passing the Civil Service examination. Again, one finds contrast with Gibbon, whose city experiences were so unhappy, and who failed to find humour or colour in Glasgow or London. Gunn played football, saw Gilbert and Sullivan, listened to atheist speakers at Marble Arch, and took to socialism 'as a duckling to water'. But, like Gibbon, he was not to rest with the conclusions of Darwin and Huxley or to be more than excited by Wells and Shaw. And typically looking at himself with detachment in the last parts of *The Atom of Delight*, he sees that:

> there he was though he was never all there, for this would pass . . . for the boy who did not belong to London. Though involved he was forever a spectator, so memory sees him as curiously anonymous and in this anonymity there was a freedom so intangible that it could hardly be touched.

In Gunn there are always more important issues than the here-and-now. He can evoke concrete detail and psychological verisimilitude (for example, the detail of a boy's poaching expedition) superbly, but it is always that intangible atom of delight or freedom, that quality of 'the other landscape' of 'the fourth dimension' which intrigues him.

Compare the superb opening fight between the boy and salmon in *Highland River* with the chapter called 'The Boy and the

Salmon' in *The Atom of Delight*. Nearly twenty years separates them, yet clearly the autobiographical incident of about 1900 has lived in the mind not so much for the fact of catching a big fish, but for what it has revealed of the deeper self. Underlying all Gunn's work is the statement of *The Atom*, the point of departure — 'I came upon myself sitting there'.

His quest is for *self*; what makes *a* self, what evidence can we find that we as humans have identity, value, permanence, immortality? In this lies apparent paradox. The writer who stresses more than anyone else the need of humanity for warmth and loyalty of community has as his other great theme the theme of essential loneliness. A comparison with Gibbon's picture of the essential loneliness of Chris Guthrie in *Grey Granite*, resolves the paradox. Chris retreats into herself. Her age and her need for community is past. Gunn's central figures from Hugh Macbeth to Finn MacHamish retreat into themselves in order to identify themselves, to draw a circle around what they essentially are. Having done so, having established their internal house of peace, they emerge to participate the more fully, since they now understand the need of others for similar identity and wholeness. One must find oneself out of the un-individuated experience of childhood, through danger, loneliness and delight; and then return that self to community. Conversely, in the later novels from *The Green Isle of the Great Deep* to *The Shadow* and *Bloodhunt*, Gunn sees attack on this sense of self as the cardinal social crime, and increasingly prevalent and dangerous after the Second World War.

The Atom of Delight places Gunn's discovery of self in London between 1906 and 1908. Surprisingly, in Edinburgh, where he finished his Civil Service income-tax training (1908–10), Gunn was far less happy than in London. *The Lost Glen, The Drinking Well* and *The Key of the Chest* show Gunn's dislike of Edinburgh social life. But he passed his exams, and from 1911–21 worked with the Customs and Excise Service all over the Highlands. With four brothers in the war, Gunn decided not to join up, and was given the job of charting shipping around and through the German submarines in the Minch. He was 'home' again. From now on Gunn's life was of a piece. He and his novelist friend Maurice Walsh worked together in singularly pleasant places, with opportunities galore for fishing, hunting, camping, and endless discussion of Scottish

15

politics, a way of life unchanged by Gunn's marriage in 1921. Gunn was active (behind the scenes, being a Civil Servant!) in the rise of the Scottish National Movement, becoming immensely respected as bridgemaker in 1932 between the two separate nationalist movements, as healer of divisions and as quiet suggester of contructive ideas of Highland regeneration.

John MacCormick, in an account of Scottish Nationalism, *The Flag in the Wind*, recalls that Gunn's Inverness house was by the late 'twenties the unofficial headquarters of the northern movement, and a 'spiritual home', 'not in any narrow and bitter nationalism'. But when MacCormick withdrew from the movement and the second war gave a bitter taste to ideas of nationalism, Gunn bowed out. The interest in social externals of the 'twenties and 'thirties, mirrored in the novels from *The Grey Coast* to *The Silver Darlings* (1926–1941), gave way to his deepest inclination, which was the pursuit of the essential self, the 'other landscape'.

There was always in Gunn the tendency to escape from the modern and 'outer' world. Typically he made his most important break *before* he knew in 1937 that he was the winner of the Tait Black prize for *Highland River*, and thus a celebrity. With war looming, and a sense of 'political terror' in the air, the purges of 1937–38 in Russia worried him even more in psychological than political terms. Gunn decided to be off, and *Off in a Boat* (1938) is the delightful story of the impulsive giving up of a secure job and house for 'a boat in doubtful condition' with 'a defective twenty-five-year-old Kelvin engine', blessed with promises of an almanac from the novelist George Blake, a small cannon 'for popping-off German submarines' from Frank Morley, a keg of rum from T. S. Eliot (all his publishers) — and a flush toilet!

This period 'at sea' was to lead to Gunn's understanding of the sea in *The Silver Darlings*. But with the coincidence of horror and delight which Gunn conveys as the nature of life in all his fiction, the other origin of the adventure lay in a domestic accident which caused Daisy's baby to be still-born. It seems to me that here one can find the love, touched with sympathy, which Gunn has for the child as archetype, and the reason why he creates childhood so vividly. And from now on, as in *Wild Geese Overhead* (1939), Gunn sees 'escape' as essential rather than escapist, and his novels picture protagonists healing themselves by doing what he has done,

16

by *not* being dominated by the idea of urban and social duty.

Gunn thenceforward earned his living as a writer, living always north of Inverness. In Strathglass in 1950 Gunn discovered Ouspensky's *In Search of the Miraculous*; this and an increasing interest in Zen Buddhism moved his last fiction into what critics have called 'mysticism', but which Gunn saw as the logical and sensible end of a quest for the sources of intellect and feeling and the source of spiritual light. Accompanying this esoteric quest was a decision to find a freedom from the 'literary world'. He wrote little from 1954 on, and died in 1973.

Gunn began with a view of Scotland which was pessimistic. His first two novels are *The Grey Coast* and *The Lost Glen* (which appeared in 1929 in serial form in *The Scots Magazine*). In the first Gunn looked at the grey outlook for the northern coasts now that the fishing had fallen away, and in the second — the only one of his novels with an unrelievedly tragic ending — he regarded with some cynicism the effects on Highland community of absentee landlords who clear their land for hunting and fishing.

The Grey Coast is a picture of a dying economy. The imagery of greyness in walls, sky and mood parallels the spiritual greyness felt by the central characters. Unlike Gunn's later work, the grey is deliberately monotone, deliberately washing colour and life out of place and character. Ironically, Gunn contrasts the facile rosy-tints of the 'Celtic Twilight' view of the peasant with the schoolmaster's inability to find anything but dogged surliness in local Gaelic culture. Much of the novel is set in night time, with suffocating walls hiding the sly approaches of person to person. Poverty and distrust have made them so. But even here Gunn's essential affirmation finds scope, for he handles the love affair of Maggie and Ivor, the poor fisherman with nothing to offer her, with rare delicacy, showing that underneath the things they can't say lie the deeper, trapped sources of their love. Their spirit may be 'grey', but there is light underneath. So also is Maggie's miser uncle, whose furtive slyness turns out to mask an unexpected humour and humanity. His money, left to Maggie, gives hope to the lovers, and although there is nothing of the idea of regeneration beginning at home which triumphantly marks the later novels, light triumphs over the powerfully drawn lowland intruder Daun Tullach, whose

17

sick desires and psychology Gunn portrays in the *Green Shutters* tradition.

The Grey Coast's faults lie in overdrawn pessimism, and this is also the case with *The Lost Glen*, an even darker study. Ewan, returned in disgrace from the city, fails to find (as the protagonists of *The Grey Coast* found) that buried and peasant strength which is the last resort of so many of Gunn's suffering heroes. Gunn widened his view of the Highlands here, looking at present political and social issues as they are embodied in a number of characters: Colonel Hicks, the first of a line of bombastic and hollow representatives of an English ruling class which is usually absent from its estates; the Union organiser who fruitlessly argues socialism against the Colonel; the 'land revolutionaries' of Ardbeg, the crofters who want a new deal; and Clare, the girl who has come to the Highlands for personal reinvigoration.

Gunn has an ambivalent attitude towards the Highlands at this time. Clare and Ewan present two opposing visions: Clare seeing her retreat to Ardbeg as regenerative and healing, a fruitful escape from modern stress; Ewan seeing the spirit of his race, 'the play and the sparkle of the spirit in music and fun and work', now reduced and degraded. Ewan turns in bitterly upon himself, symbolically destroying himself and the Colonel in the sea. The symbolism may be crude but there is deep and sensitive irony, seen in the devastating satiric picture of the local concert, with the holidaying aristocracy condescending to 'their' locals and boasting of them to their visitors. The locals speak in two tongues: in dry and critical Gaelic, drawing their dislike into a shared and sly undercurrent, and posing through their bright English as parodic and dutiful peasants. Gunn puts his finger on the deepest malaise of the native Gael.

Morning Tide marks the rebirth of Gunn's affirmative vision. It is a novel set in Gunn's own village, and echoes of *The Grey Coast* pervade it. Life at sea claims lives — as we see, dramatically — and the fishing is dying. Alan Macbeth (the name implying 'son of Dunbeath') emigrates with friends in the central movement of the book. Lives are poor, and the mother wishes for university or a white-collar job for her sons. So where is the hope? It is presented for the first time in the figure of the boy, Hugh Macbeth. In his initiation into life we follow a rhythm of irrepressible hope. The outside rhythms are those of a passing way of life, the internal pulse is Hugh's and indomitable. Gunn is 'growing up' in his own spirit through the imagined response of Hugh to Gunn's own experience.

This is done by finding the lowest point (as Gunn had done in *The Lost Glen*), accepting that the fight may be unsuccessful, and yet fighting still. Old Hector, the centre for ceilidhs and talk and fun, and the anticipation of the later 'Old Hector', expresses this:

> 'Never give in to the thing when it's coming at you. And at the worst — at the worst —'
> Alan leapt to his feet with a laugh.
> 'At the worst, battened down and with sails set — sail her right under!'

The major achievement of the book is the realisation of the boy's consciousness, with the evocation of his family and place. When we first meet Hugh he has crossed a boundary between childhood and adolescence. He has been sent to gather bait when he could have been playing football. Gunn perceptively catches the struggle in the mind, the mixture of pride and feeling hard done to, with the growing sense that what he is doing on the lonely beach *matters*, so that he will defy the taunts of Rid Jock and fight him *for his self*, his new sense of manhood. More, he begins to sense the tensions at home, the unstated fear of his mother that Alan will want to go to sea — as he does — and the adult sexual tensions between his sisters and their lover, Charlie Chisholm, so that he can walk a delicate line, understanding Grace's repressed tension and Kirstie's passionate outbursts where he couldn't before. By the time of the great storm which ends the first part he is ready to comfort his distraught mother, and he is already a replacement for his father and brother if the worst should happen. The first part ends instead with a superb description in Gunn's most vivid action narrative of Hugh's father and friends conquering the storm through sheer skill and courage.

Hugh has several tests to go through. He must fight for his sister Kirstie's honour, clarifying in his mind why it is he liked her more than Grace. His instinct is right, Kirstie the warm-hearted and guileless and stay-at-home having the essence of the community's spirit, where Grace (artful grace) is only home on a visit, a servant to gentry, already displaced in her values, 'superior'. Hugh sees too for the first time the figure of his mother as archetype, of the Earth, enduring her illness. Suffering clarifies vision; Hugh sees the strengths and the weaknesses of his community, the comfort to be gained from religion in the reading of the psalms when the mother appears to be dying, and its other side, its repression of the peoples' traditional love of fun and song and poaching.

Gunn has put darkness behind him. But he has a mammoth task ahead. He sets out now to diagnose, through creative acts of historic imagination, to present the spiritual history of the Gael, with their strengths and weaknesses, and to present through story, legend and myth a picture of possible regeneration.

He does this in four novels between 1933 and 1946. They are *Sun Circle* (1933), *Butcher's Broom* (1934), *Highland River* (1937) and *The Silver Darlings* (1941).

The setting for *Sun Circle* is that of *Morning Tide* — Dunbeath strath, but over a thousand years ago. The connection between novels is clear. Gunn is now going back to the beginnings of the Strath people, when the Raven tribe led by Drust and his lady, Silis, live in relative peace and much liveliness and humour as children of the Druid. They are a shore-and-moor people, worshipping Light in their Sun Circles of stone. History has reached one of what Yeats would call its 'gyres'. Christianity has appeared and is tolerated — even encouraged — in the glen, in the person of the good St Molrua, one of St Columba's missionaries of Celtic Christianity from Iona.

Gunn's people are civilisers, not conquerors. Here Gunn is close to Gibbon's 'Antique Scene' verdict; that the Picts were a cultured, peaceful people. Their Druid Master sees the coming tragedy in the almost childish glee of the Ravens in seeing adventure in the coming of the Vikings. They are sure of victory over them and the Logenmen, their local rivals:

> At a time when a great decision has to be made, a decision to go forward, to conquer... they feel that by going forward they leave their true riches behind ... the instinct for that is in them, and acts like a nerveless infirmity of the will. They can go forward, but it is for something that no leader could

ever understand.... There is thus in them a profound persistence.

There is a goodness in such a people, in their delight in community rather than the separation of leadership. All their fun and love of complex intricacy in art and talk depends on communality. Their riches are their lives, not their ambitions. They are easily defeated by the Vikings, who are amazed at their guileless lack of cover on the beach. Their relationship with Nature is open, like their frank whole acceptance of fleshy sexuality *and* spiritual simplicity. But they then believe too readily Molrua the missionary's dramatic contrast of Spirit and Flesh, Heaven and Hell, Good and Evil. They are like Golding's simple folk meeting subtle man in *The Inheritors*, with the added tragedy that the art of *these* people is far from simple, and far beyond the achievement of their conquerors.

Gunn also shows a pair of the tribe, Aniel and Breeta, facing local choices. Aniel is drawn to the fair Nessa and the dark Breeta (shades of Grace and Kirstie in *Morning Tide*); and his choice of Breeta is important. She is the earth, enduring like Maggie in *The Grey Coast*, the mother in *Morning Tide*, and Gunn's finest such symbol, Dark Mairi of the Shore in *Butcher's Broom*. Aniel and Breeta go off after tragedy has wrecked the tribe. Drust has been killed, his wife is dead by her own hand, his daughter Nessa burned by the tribe in the sun circle because she has united with the Viking leader Haakon. But the killing of Nessa and Haakon does not cancel in our minds the thought Gunn has planted — that in union between invaded and invader is the origin of the mingling of Pict and Norse which so clearly did happen from Orkney to Aberdeen. Molrua is killed beside his chapel. (Is this or the Master the ghostly figure Finn 'sees' in the house of peace?) But his death is meant to imply a martyrdom which if anything will bring Christianity the more quickly. The Druid Master dies, but sees racial survival nevertheless:

> For tragedy had come upon this place and upon them all. But that was not an end. Tragedy may kill an individual, but it does not kill a people.

21

Aniel is the Master's favourite pupil. In his survival with Breeta the elemental spirit goes on. For as Young Art will carry on the knowledge of Old Hector, so Aniel will take something of the Druid and Pictish past which will never be entirely lost.

Sun Circle's action prefigures later history. The relationship of Drust and Silis will be repeated in that of Malcolm Canmore and 'Margaret the Good', in the woman's encouragement of Christianity and discouragement of deepest tradition. The peculiar inability to assert or go forward as a conquering unit which causes the tribe to fail in the face of a pragmatic enemy will recur throughout Scotland's history, especially affecting the society of *Butcher's Broom* through the Highland failure in 1745, and persisting till the present day.

In Molrua's introduction of war between matters spiritual and fleshly we see the origin of Presbyterianism and its condemnation of the Highlanders when they suffer the Clearances. And the guilt induced by this distinction will fester through centuries, and already, in the adoption of the chief's son, reared in the south, as 'imported' leader, the great betrayals of the eighteenth and nineteenth centuries are anticipated.

Butcher's Broom is the sequel. A thousand years lie between the times of these novels. The significance of this is that the forces released by the breaking of *Sun Circle* have merged and lived in comparative harmony for that millenium. The effect of 'Butcher' Cumberland's 'broom' after Culloden in 1745 is the next huge upheaval. Gunn begins with an extended description of the inland strath, the Riasgan, where the descendants of *Sun Circle* live in the benevolent care of the Captain, their blood-connection with their absent chief in London. He presents a texture of rich lore and humorous recreation of ceilidh, crofting activity, and varied characterisation, and a bleak description of betrayal. Gunn has deep bitterness about this betrayal in this novel and his careful structure and pacing of events is designed partly to distance that bitter intensity (to avoid the trap of overstatement that Gibbon so often falls into) and partly to increase *our* feeling of anger, as without appreciation of the *quality* of this ancient community culture our regret must inevitably be diminished.

Evil and betrayal emanate from two sources — the chief and the church:

The modern landlords trusted not only to the power of the church and state behind them, but to their privileged position as chiefs of their clansmen. It was a betrayal impossible, perhaps unthinkable — to Viking or Druid; and, bewildered and broken, the people were driven to the seashores without lifting a hand in their own defence. There was no question here of lack of courage, for at that very time men from these glens were winning renown in the armies of Britain in Europe, Africa and America. In their act of betrayal, the chiefs risked nothing and won everything. Yet the chiefs did risk something; they risked any spiritual reason for their existence and lost it for ever.

The betrayal is in three parts, with the first part conveying the peculiar relationship of people and place. Landscape is seen through these people's eyes as almost human. They conceive of land-use in a way which intuitively values the land *for itself*, but also as part of themselves. Their language mixes categories of human and animal and natural, so that we come to see that there is a wholeness here whereby the Riasgan, like *Highland River's* strath, is an entity where animal, human and landscape are one and animate together. Dark Mairi represents this wholeness, with her wordless but ancient communion with plant and herb, with her basket with elements of sea and land in it. She is healer and descendant of the ancient Druids, ignoring (without rudeness) the talk of the minister Bannerman because to her it is irrelevant. Her death will mark the passing of the Riasgan as an entity.

And beyond her Gunn marvellously evokes the lives of the people. Their trust is clearly stated:

> The Captain's duty was to supply his chief with men and otherwise to assist him in the maintenance of his position . . . . the people of the Riasgan, because they liked the Captain, still followed the ancient labour custom with natural enough grace. Profoundly within them there might even be a secret pleasure in doing the Captain's work, a satisfaction arising out of the idea of pure service directed towards someone higher than themselves, for the Captain was the blood representative of the chief, and the chief was father to them all.

There is something ominous in the vulnerable openness of such thought. Men can be used, if supplied, for many things; and 'fatherly' chiefs are suspect. But even when the chief uses their rents to pay 'debts of honour' in London they still 'retain in him some of the magical conception of the chief, so deep did their ways of life run and from so ancient a source'.

We are not yet, however, in the Clearances. The ground is being softened up for them, with Pitt the Younger's clever stroke of using the best of the young men (otherwise troublesome as in 1715 and 1745) for British wars overseas. The young men, like Elie's lover Colin, are drawn to the bait, encouraged by the church. Women are left unprotected; Clearance will be easy. And the third part, with its contrast of 'civilised' discussion in London in the chief's magnificently furnished house (with its Highlanders in full regalia at the front door) and the squalid atrocities of the actual evictions, completes the undoing of a thousand years of culture. Anticipating *The Green Isle of the Great Deep*, the central theme emerges of the horror of destroying man's essence:

> ... we did not blame them for murdering the body; we blamed them for murdering the soul; we blamed them for taking an order of mankind, faithful and loyal, who in the course of ages had given light to the world and ... great music and story; for having taken that order to which they themselves belonged, and for thirty fleeces of wool to have betrayed it in its own garden and destroyed it.

Dark Mairi is torn to pieces by the sheepdogs, with her grandson looking on. But some hope is seen in the return of Colin from the wars. He kills the dogs and saves his own son and takes Mairi's body to the shore — where *The Silver Darlings* will take up, using MacHamish, the name of a Riasgan hero, as the name of its hero and his greater son. Thus life will come from death.

Thematically the novel is brilliantly conceived in terms of opposing sets of values and concepts. Thus with 'culture'; for the aptly named factor responsible for the Clearances, Heller (based on Patrick Sellars) continually imputes to the Riasgan a barbarism which he as a lowlander sees because he knows nothing of the language or music of the people. His friends see the natives as 'ignorant, lazy and filthy', talking 'gibberish'. They conclude that 'their dialect can have only a few words, because the things around them are few and they live pretty much like animals...'. But in the opening pages we read:

> the old language Mairi used was full of such names, not only for things but for men; particularly, indeed for men, so that the name evokes each kind of man with an astonishing, almost laughable, magic. Naturally with this go diminutives that are the finger tips of fun, phrases that snare the heart with a hair. For love-making, it is a subtle tongue... immensely old.

Notice the slip into the present tense, for this is also the Gaelic of now, only richer still then. We see that the visitors' English is clipped and restrictive, the language of barter, materialism and legal destruction of a race. *They*, as so often in the work of Gibbon, are the barbarians.

The economic and social 'strength' of these men is contrasted with the loving 'strength' of Mairi and Elie, enduring womens' strength, or Rob's or MacHamish's vivid physical power. Their corrosive ambition and jealousy is contrasted with the healthier relationships of the people of the Riasgan, who are subtle in their dealings, but cannot hold poison for any length of time within them.

Another thematic contrast is between the Riasgan's pagan joy in dance, song, and fun and the new reproving strictures of the church. Here Thomas the drover speaks for the old ways, using irony and 'blasphemy' of a hilarious kind to undercut the pompous utterances of Bannerman the minister. Thomas's prediction of the coming of the Great Beast, the Satan he's heard promised from the pulpit as punishment for the folk's sins, is both riotously funny and ominously accurate. He parodies Bannerman's 'message' from St John, delighting and disturbing his inebriate friends with his conclusion that the Great Beast is a cheviot ewe! But is he not right? And the church fails the people. There is good intention within the minister's heart, but his restriction of life's totality of flesh and spirit to the spirit, his artificial categories of good and bad, and his final support for the landlords, destroys his integrity and his community.

In the end we're left with two poignant images. The great pibroch 'Lament for the children', which haunted *Morning Tide*, haunts this novel. At its heart lies a scene of great power, when the heartbroken wife of the Captain, anticipating the doom of the Riasgan and her kinsfolk, destroys the shrub, badge and honour of her clan. I suggested at the beginning of my discussion that the title came from the name of a heartless enemy of the Highlander. We see now another significance. The shrub which was traditionally used in healing is now of no consequence:

> Slowly she withdrew the piece of shrub from the jar and gazed at it. 'In the Latin this box-holly is called Ruscus Aculeatus.' She turned her face to him (the Captain). 'Do you know what it's called in English? He stared at her. 'No'. 'Butcher's Broom,' she said. From the moment's obliterating irony she turned away, and with a quiet gesture threw the shrub in the fire.

Gunn also uses the Christian statement which Chris Guthrie utters at the end of *Cloud Howe*: 'It is finished'. The difference between the two usages comes out in the fact that where Chris draws an end to Robert's and a people's right to use Christian symbolism or faith any longer, Gunn asks a question: 'When tragedy thus completes itself has it not earned in a people the dignity of saying 'It is finished'?'

For Gunn it is not finished. There is both worse and better to come, and the course of his fiction is to find a way of accepting and transcending such change. (Again, one notes that Gibbon's response after reading Gunn was to forget 'aesthetic appreciations' and to be 'filled with anger and pity for those people of yours — detachment in these matters is impossible for me. I'm too close to these folk myself. GREAT BOOK.') Gunn's movement towards acceptance brought a change of direction in 1937.

Highland River tells us that he is moving on to explore the inner, as well as the outer, landscape. After acknowledging the connection with *Morning Tide* he sums up the essential difference. The hunts, the forays after rabbits and salmon are concrete and actual, but they are also part of the mature novelist's other hunt — 'a poaching expedition to the source of delight', as his foreword calls it.

Highland River and the spiritual autobiography *The Atom of Delight* (1937 and 1954) are the first and last great statements of the theme of the significance of the moment of delight, round which the other novels revolve. Nowhere else does he enunciate so clearly his central ideas, although one must immediately qualify this by adding that *The Silver Darlings* is a more complete and satisfying work of art. *Highland River* marks the deepening and intensifying point in Gunn's own flow of development and deserves inclusion amongst his greatest novels for several reasons: because it sings his major theme of delight; because it introduces motifs and symbols like those of serpent and circle which will recur throughout his work; because, in its complex but extremely satisfying structure and time sequence, it shows Gunn the deliberate artist experimenting in a manner reminiscent of Proust or Virginia Woolf with the entire methodology of the novel form; and finally because as a result of all these he produces a magnificent, if not unflawed, *Prelude*-like account, somewhere between the novel and the long poem, of the growth of a sensitive mind to the point where it finds itself. It is Gunn's portrait of the artist as a young man. Yet is it typical of his humility that he should portray Kenn — so close to himself — first as one of the folk, and second as a scientist, devoid of Stephen Daedalus's (or James Joyce's!) egotism about the special nature of the artist.

The best way into this rich and complex work is to follow the image and the idea of the river itself. Since Gunn talks of finding delight's source, exploration of this river will reveal just what Gunn's theme is; the river is to this novel what the image and idea of the circle and the ring of stones known as the House of Peace is to *The Silver Darlings*. It runs through the novel from first chapter to last. We move from the sea it joins, to the populated places round its mouth, to the crofting country higher up its banks, to the lonelier Pict and pagan haunted places close to the moors, and finally on to the bare, eternally desolate moors in which the river has its source.

This is a real river in a real strath, with real salmon. As Gunn reminds us, Kenn 'was hunting nothing abstract. The "salmon of knowledge" for him had real silver scales and a desirable shape; the eyes he feared were the telescope eyes of gamekeepers.' On this real level Gunn has no superiors at evoking seasonal change in a country landscape. Read Chapter VI alone with its description of the stormy winter; of the sea thundering on the beach 'with reverberations that would be heard far inland'; of the dim afternoon light where drizzle thickens into rain, where the drop at the end of an old woman's nose is 'distilled from misery's final self'. The river in this chapter takes on its own cruel power, has 'a submerged sound of grinding boulders' as it boils and seethes.

But one must broaden the river's scope to include the entire strath and its creatures, since they are so interconnected. Gunn describes an animal landscape which merges with the physical (including the humans) without extra respect for any part of the whole. The way this is done is by describing Kenn and his fellows in animal metaphors. As a boy, in winter, Kenn curls up in bed:

> It was great fun to be so safe in this warm hole, while the dark cold river rolled on its way to the distant thunder of the sea . . . . animals, furry and warm, were curled up in their dens . . . curled up, like himself, and heard, waking or in sleep the rushing of the river . . . . The picture made him snuggle in his own den, and smell the thick warmth out of his own pelt.

Thus Kenn and Beel and Art are creatures in a landscape; they sniff 'with the action of a stag'; their cheeks are 'petals of the dogrose'; their eyes are 'quicker than tits or finches'. Chapter XV has at its centre a 'stream of consciousness' representing animal states of mind, immediately savouring smells, tastes and glimpses of summer. In a pool, Beel is a water-rat, Kenn a seal; they are as persistent as otters; they dam the pool like beavers.

Gunn also uses the converse. Human terms are applied to natural phenomena. Kenn listens to the river and hears a heart beating: 'contract and expand, systole and diastole; the river flows'. There is the evocation in lonely places of a presence which animates the landscape, not merely the threat of the keepers, but something which can be glimpsed in the inhuman but more than animal eye of a gull, or:

> that inexplicable sensation of there being an eye about somewhere, a non-human eye, a peat-hag eye under heather tufts.

Gunn emphasises the animal in the human, and the more than animal or merely physical in the landscape behind the human. Thus the salmon, which comes from the dark continental shelf of the Atlantic at the stirrings of some long-sleeping instinct to enter the fresh-water currents of the river to explore the remote reaches from which he once came, is a parallel to Kenn, with instinctive quest by both for the source. In Chapter II the continental ledge, that deep water in which the salmon passes his unthinking existence, is used as a metaphor for Kenn's mind. Kenn and the salmon are in the middle stages of their development. They have as yet no thought of exploring for the source, but are content to move unthinking at a level of sensual enjoyment. Remembering this much later:

> here the grown-up Kenn pauses because it was this very point of what the salmon may feel at such a moment (the moment when the salmon begins his search for the source) that first launched him on this search into lost times.

Kenn the adult will search for his source like the salmon, as when, with the boys, going upriver, they:

> came to the base of an overhanging rock with a slanting passageway to either hand, as salmon might come to a pool where two rivers meet. Which way now? They had no memory of ever having chosen before. Yet they hardly hesitated, all three going to the left. And if one had gone to the right, he would very soon have sniffed and returned, just as an old salmon has been known to go a short distance up one stream, then inexplicably to return and follow the other, that, unknown to him, had been chosen of his brethren for thousands of years.

Later as a soldier he is beset by horror and death; and he is sustained by this kinship with the animal. The 'action of a salmon', 'cool river cunning', instinctively saves him when he's blinded by gas on the Somme.

Time and again the movement of Kenn's mind, as it flashes with delight or takes refuge deep within itself, is expressed in this salmon metaphor. In old Celtic symbolism the salmon is the salmon of wisdom, eating the hazelnuts of knowledge which drop into the pools of the river of life. In this early novel Gunn does not develop this symbolism to the level at which it operates in, say, *The Green Isle of the Great Deep*; but Kenn is gathering knowledge and becoming one with the salmon of wisdom.

The salmon should also be seen in another light: linked with the river and somehow marvellous, in the same way as other beautiful, surprising and elusive creatures are seen. 'Magical' is a word which Gunn associates with this kind of animal or creature, in the sense that nature only rarely vouchsafes their appearance, let alone their entire presence, as a gift. Thus the sighting of a *black* rabbit, the discovery of the sudden grace of hinds at the source of the river or the catching of the salmon itself. There is great skill in the weaving together of these animal glimpses or events which occur as Kenn moves upriver through his boyhood. They are motifs, central images, ideas, phrases even, which as they are re-used and recur take on a deeper significance. Kenn's response to the same motif changes as he develops. By recognising the motif we are not only able to measure the extent of his development, but time is momentarily cancelled out, and we are simultaneously aware of every other occasion on which Kenn hunted salmon, tried to trap linnets, or felt the presence of desolate places. It takes a little while to realise the method, since obviously Gunn has first to state his motifs, the images and ideas which will later be echoed or varied. The most obvious example is in the recurrence of the pool; the Well pool at the beginning gives way to the higher Achglas pool, which gives way to the Lodge pool even higher, till the final small loch at the end. Each has its separate character, yet they are linked. We recognise Kenn's spiritual progress at each new pool, and we remember with a sense of timelessness the smaller and younger Kenns.

This kind of juxtaposition of separate times forms the very texture of the novel. When Kenn learns very early that Leicester is famous for boots, we read this firstly as a part of a sensitive condemnation by Gunn of the teaching of inert, unrelated facts. The children do not get taught local, vivid folk-history, or anything of the culture which relates to their lives; they learn the lives of long-dead English kings. The passage is self-sufficient, but Gunn weaves it into a bigger pattern by having it echoed years later in the hospital where Kenn, blinded by gas, finds a moment of ironic delight when he realises he *is* in Leicester. The memory, as he murmurs the old school lesson to himself, takes him back to the strath. Time is cancelled by delight, his deafness from shell noise clears, and he hears the rumble of hospital noise as 'the far cry of brown water in the hollow of a strath'. Even then the motif is not finished, as the nurse who tends him there recurs at the end; he is still in touch with her, and we are still in touch with several moments of Kenn's life simultaneously.

Another motif is that of the presence, the strange and sometimes threatening life within the inanimate world. The boy is conscious of it in an empty house; he sees it later in a gull's eye, where the eye seems to be that of more than gull, the very spirit of wilderness, 'wild and cold and watchful'; and he will find on his poaching expeditions that more than the keepers have eyes. The motif runs all through — and thus it is the climax to this when he finds, in maturity, he fears neither the darkness nor the watching eyes. The use of the motif enables us to realise his coming to maturity.

People are at once themselves — mother, father, brother — and motifs. The father's 'Bless me, boy' occurs at beginning and end as a phrase, the same in its warm kindliness, but subtly different in the way it relates to Kenn's development. The father himself has shrunk through the course of time from bearded giant and benevolent patriarch, to a man, dignified but somehow more vulnerable. The mother too, is real, yet part of a recurrent pattern of archetypal womanhood; the nurse, the old woman who is considered by Kenn the fittest human being to represent the race to God, even the young girl Annie, all are linked, deliberately, by recurrence of descriptive phrase and image to a central figure who is simply Woman. None of Kenn's family or friends is presented in the usual narrative fashion, but they emerge before us in moments which, while exceptionally graphic in the amount they tell us about them as individuals, are nevertheless important primarily in that they develop previous moments.

The main characteristic of these motifs, these groups of linked episodes, is that they are carefully chosen *moments*. The word is not trivial for Gunn. It is probably the most used word in all his work, and certainly so in this novel. What Gunn is doing in *Highland River* is picking moments of delight and wonder from

31

Kenn's childhood and adolescence, moments which will contribute towards his central revelation.

Sometimes the repeated image becomes so strongly indicative of the theme that it has become more than motif, but symbol in itself. The salmon takes on this extra dimension, and at the end the hinds are symbolic of the same meaning. The bird motif also develops into the specific symbol of delight, the green linnet; while curlews, peewits and gulls haunt the book, ever present at the back of Kenn's consciousness as he wanders through the strath. The green linnet *is* the elusive moment of delight; it is the one bird that Kenn has never caught, only glimpsed. Even more than salmon or hind, there is something particularly apt in the use of the bird to symbolise the fleeting, unpredictable point in time when sheer delight is glimpsed.

We are, it must be realised, still within the central river theme of the work. But now the river has taken on even wider scope. It is now quite deliberately meant by Gunn to be a river of time and of space. By using the motif method, Gunn can place us as he wishes at any and several of the branches and pools which are the significant developing points in Kenn's life. Gunn refers throughout to 'straths of the past', and develops the notion that Kenn the adult, in deliberately remembering his past, is moving up a river of time. As Kurt Wittig says in *The Scottish Tradition in Literature*:

in *Highland River*, even in hunting the salmon as it pursues its pilgrimage between light and darkness back to the source of its life, Kenn himself is making a similar journey back to the source of his own life.

The intention is to show how the child is father of the man. Mature Kenn is actively remembering the moments which made him. Gunn must have at least a dual time-sequence since we must know two Kenns to know the relation between them. The childhood moment of delight, an intense moulding experience, is followed by an adult or adolescent experience which has somehow been conditioned by the earlier episode. The Leicester-linked passages may be seen as an example; the scenes with Angus in childhood and then Angus in war as another, with typical attention to detail in the motif which links the two, the image of pellets of earth being displaced, first by serpent, then by rifle shot. The strath-rooted memory enables Kenn to face city squalor, war horrors, cynicism of colleagues — and himself. The effect of juxtaposing time past with time present is that time is momentarily cancelled and the river of the past rolls into Kenn's spirit, filling him with the sense of wonder and delight he needs. This river of time which knows no temporal barrier is a river in space too, for Kenn finds in France that the Somme can become his Highland river.

We change perspective yet again, and the river of memory becomes a river of humanity, of Highland folk and all their ways, stories and songs which surround Kenn. Gunn believes that for most Western people this river took a wrong turning:

> It's a far cry to the golden age, to the blue smoke of the heath fire and the scent of the Primrose! Our river took a wrong turning somewhere! But we haven't forgotten the source.

Like Gibbon, Gunn believes that primitive pre-Christian and pre-institutionalised man possessed an innocence and a communion with his organic surroundings. Kenn, in seeking the source of the real river, is not only in search of himself as a separate person but, although at first this may seem a contradition, he is also in search of his community, present and past. One is, in Gunn's view, first a clearly defined and essentially alone person, but this does not destroy the further need of the individual for family and friends and community identity. There is nothing solipsistic in Gunn's concept of the essential loneliness of man.

In searching for himself in this fuller social sense, Kenn finds the river of men, with Spartacus, Copernicus, Galileo and Leonardo da Vinci, as well as the river of fishermen and peasants. But for all these illustrious 'salmon', Kenn finds that the essence of the river is that it is of the folk. As he considers who should speak for humanity to God at the source, it is the old woman, wasted almost to pure spirit, shy and withdrawn in her cottage by the river, that he chooses.

These truths do not come at once to Kenn. He is given insight in moments of surprise or delight, as in the first chapter of the novel, when hunting the huge salmon in the Well pool:

out of that noiseless world in the grey of the morning, all his ancestors came at him. They tapped his breast until the bird inside it fluttered madly; they drew a hand along his hair until the scalp crinkled; they made the blood within him tingle to a dance that had him leaping from boulder to boulder. . . . Not only did his hunting ancestors of the Caledonian forest come at him, but his grown up brothers and his brothers' friends, with their wild forays and epic stories.

Here is Jung's 'collective unconscious' in operation. It is this inner instinct which impels Kenn upriver, giving him glimpses of the next stage, the higher value or beauty of the river of life. It is the same instinct as urged the salmon. Legends, song and story carry this ancient knowledge, which is why Gunn in all his work sets such high value on the act of story-telling or singing, or seeing and hearing the traces of the elder people in ruins of brochs.

But there is to this stream of affirmation a dark counter current, summed up in the use of the motif of the keepers. In Kenn's mind, as he hunts the salmon in the Well pool,

the fear . . . of the fish itself . . . was also infinitely complicated by fear of gamekeepers, of the horror and violence of lawcourts, of our modern social fear.

There *is* something sick in the fact that the people who have fished and hunted the strath for a millenium are now legally forbidden to do so, and that the fish and game are now the 'property' of an absentee landlord. There is much of Gibbon's feeling that the 'elder' people have been cheated, but there is nothing of Gibbon's hysteria. Compare Gibbon's treatment of the demoralisation and degradation of Ewan in *Sunset Song* with Gunn's expression of the same theme in showing how Kenn's brother Angus has been drained by the horror he has seen. There is no demonstration of Angus's debased state through acts of sadism, aided by physical description. In Gibbon's case, this is emotive, since it associates Ewan's close-cropped hair and putrescent scars with his inner fall. Instead, we juxtapose the Angus we have met at odd intervals poaching and humouring his younger brother, with the shifty-eyed new Angus, advising Kenn to take no unnecessary chances — Angus, the daredevil tree-swinger, who found in chances his delight!

Kenn tries in the trenches to relocate him in the river that matters, and not the river which has taken a wrong turning and which is guarded by keepers at every point. But the trenches' tragedy is a natural development of the earlier episode when Angus and Kenn were almost caught by the keepers. For all Angus's basic decency, he seems to lack Kenn's deeper wellsprings of strength. He is like Ronnie of *The Silver Darlings*, with an inner weakness that gives in to the pressures of the sick society. As they lay hiding from the keepers:

> Kenn looked at Angus's face. It had whitened, and playing on it was a weak surface smile.
>
> All the dark proud life was gone.
>
> Doom was in the nervous lips, in the shallow glitter of the eyes. The spirit, netted in the white smile, haunted Kenn through all the rest of his years.

This ghost-face becomes another motif of the novel. In it is prefigured Angus's spiritual defeat. He will be too weak to hold the river in his mind. Kenn is appalled by his nervous warning:

> ... take care, do no more than you must.... And all the time the river as pure memory, receding ... receding ... until their talk became forced.

The ghost-face of Angus joins the other hidden fears of the younger Kenn. Only in maturity will he fully conquer them, and in so doing conquer all threats to the river of his own development, be they the obvious assaults of Calvinism, the horrors of slums or war, or the more insidious cynicism of the scientist Radzyn.

Finally, for Gunn and for Kenn the notion of the river as a continual pouring from a source of moments of delight is the one which illuminates and unites all aspects of the river and all motifs. Here Gunn provides a reason for the river of humanity and the internal river of consciousness to flow at all. It is the moment of delight which blesses the human condition. Such moments recollected in stress or tranquility are Wordsworthian glimpses of another landscape. From *Highland River* all Gunn's novels carry a title which symbolises this place or condition of timeless harmony with all creation and with oneself, often with the added implication that this state comes as water in a parched and wasted land.

The Well at the World's End, *The Drinking Well*, *The Lost Chart*, *The Other Landscape*, *Wild Geese Overhead* — all are images drawing on this basic idea of refreshment from the 'magical' moment of delight so that all fragmentation of experience is lost and there is unity of self and surroundings. Whether one has shared this kind of experience or not is irrelevant as a basis for criticism. Gunn has felt them, and has based his aesthetic organisation on them, just as Wordsworth did in *The Prelude*. Let us look briefly at one such moment: young Kenn's capture of the huge salmon at the beginning of the novel.

To begin with, it comes as a surprise. There is a sense of wonder about the sly unpredictability of nature. Gunn has cajoled us into seeing the natural world as animate, even as possessing a sense of humour; all through, it will play such tricks on Kenn with black rabbits and green linnets and false sources for his river that mock his seriousness. At the Well pool he is sleepy, and 'as at a signal in a weird fairy tale', the world suddenly changes. The fabulous mood, the sense of comic myth, is increased by the emphasis that this huge salmon which ploughs at his feet is the 'all father of fish'; it will be a 'saga' of a fight.

The moment does more than surprise; it *develops* Kenn, since for the first time his instincts, all the memories of his race, are awakened in him. In the fight that ensues, there is nothing sentimental. The salmon is hunted remorselessly — and Kenn will accept this in wartime as his lot. Unnecessary cruelty is one thing; the facts of life another. The fight with the salmon draws out instincts for ferocity and animal cunning he did not know he possessed.

It also, afterwards, redefines his relationship with his family. His mother realises on his return with the salmon that she cannot treat him as a boy:

> ... there was a flame, an intolerant fighting spirit, that knit him together, and separated him from her in a way that suddenly pulled at her heart.

He is being individualised. He folds his achievement and the glorious memory of it to himself, thereby getting into trouble from the schoolmaster who cannot reach his privacy. In musing about the salmon Kenn *becomes* the salmon, moving from the salt depths to the freshwater river in his mind.

Increasingly, he is able to distil deeper and more personal meaning from such moments, as when he creeps into the Pictish broch and finds that time telescopes, and 'from two thousand years back time's fingers could touch them in less than an instant'. He now gathers more than simple wonder from such experiences. In maturity he feels that he has occasionally 'had an impression of very nearly visualising the fourth dimension'.

Finally, it must be realised that Gunn is moving into areas normally discussed in religious terms. Already perhaps affected by Zen Buddhist and Taoist philosophies, he leaves the conclusion of *Highland River* open, but the implications point to a God who vouchsafes us these moments when all leaps into significance. The animism which moves in trees and hills and makes Kenn aware of a presence is not merely attributable to projection on Kenn's part. This way, Gunn seems to hint, lies God — no Christian God, indeed a God of no creed whatever, but the conscious source of the river of delight. We never see him; Kenn's final vision at the source is private, and perhaps this is as it must be — that we should be taken, enthralled, to the final mystery, and left wondering.

After *Highland River* Gunn evolves towards a novel in which social and economic problems become less important than the problem of the individual's quest for harmony in a world Gunn increasingly sees as threatened by man's will to social power. It was after *Highland River* that he took 'off in a boat' because of his dislike of political tendencies in Russia and Germany. Even in his next masterpiece, *The Silver Darlings*, one can clearly detect that the earlier motif of destructive Authority has become enlarged. Here it becomes the vast symbol of impersonal power which crushes the shore community, the tall navy ship and the pressgang which destroy Tormad and, more significantly for Gunn's future development, remove the essence of self from Ronnie, who returns as spent and washed out in mind, just as the victims of the Questioners in *The Green Isle of the Great Deep* are 'cleansed'.

I deal with *The Silver Darlings* in depth in Chapter Five as climax to this study. Suffice it here to 'place' it at this point in Gunn's development as the point of balance between the earlier 'epic of Scotland' novels and the later quests for harmony of self. It is concrete *and* metaphysical, a historic picture and a timeless symbolic representation of man's work and art on land and sea. Gunn committed himself of this novel as to no other, reading works like Anson's *Fishing Boats and Fisher Folk on the East Coast of Scotland* and fishermen's ledgers of the period, meeting fishermen who remembered their voyages past the Butt of Lewis, going with them to the Flannan Isles, and finding out about the plague coming to Caithness. 1937–1941 is obviously given over to the great work. But alongside this gestatory period there is, oddly, a feeling, evident in the surrounding novels, of unsureness and indirection. Yes, he knows entirely where *The Silver Darlings* is going; but what then?

Three novels show this uncertainty: *Wild Geese Overhead* (1939), *Second Sight* (1940) and *The Drinking Well* (1946). The first two are Gunn's least effective novels. *Wild Geese* is not at home in its city environment and its coy love affair. *Second Sight* comes dangerously close to the John Buchan and *John MacNab* cliche situation of the hunting party and its privileged conversations, affairs and challenges — with Gunn for once coming close to condecension to his second-sighted peasants, as his upper-class visitors debate their noble but savage spirituality.

The Serpent is a much better novel than these, with important statements about Gunn's beliefs. But it is too like Fionn MacColla's *The Albannach* (1932) and his own *The Lost Glen*, looking backward in its repetition of the story of 'the man who came back', just as *The Drinking Well* again repeats the theme of city failure, retreat to country and spiritual regeneration. The sense of tired repetition is heightened here by Gunn's for once frenetic addition of an improbable ending, where a rich American 'deus ex machina' saves the hero and Highland future.

These novels suggest a hiatus, a shift of approach in Gunn's work caused by the Second World War. Lest we gain the impression of loss of creativity, however, it must be remembered that at the same time that one strain of fiction was dying, another of astonishing power was emerging in *Young Art and Old Hector* (1942) and its sequel, *The Green Isle of the Great Deep* (1944). Sadly, space does not allow more than a brief indication of the achievement of this masterpiece.

The two can be read separately, but should be read as one. The first is a collection of episodes that appear to be short stories about a boy, Art, and his close, delicate relationship with an old man, Hector. But, remembering *Highland River's* emphasis on 'the moment of delight', we can see that these are not separate stories but cumulative epiphanies. Through these carefully arranged and progressive adventures, from being the youngest brother left behind weeping as his elders go off 'to the river', place of all life and unattainable adventure to the boy, he matures with the help of wise Hector's stories and diplomacy till he saves his friends from the hated 'gaugers', the government officers out to stop the illicit stills and to capture the makers of illegal whisky.

Young Art shows with great sensitivity the *quality* of a community. Beyond this overt description lies Gunn's quest for the river; for *Young Art* is organised around the idea of the river of magic and life towards which Art is nudging throughout. Like the young King Arthur he represents, his Grail is the source of delight, the river is his starting point, and Hector (like wise Sir Hector) is the river watcher and guardian of the boy's spiritual progress from knowledge to wisdom.

Young Art and Old Hector ends with Hector at last on his way to the river with Art. We don't see them arrive; that is kept as sequel in *The Green Isle*, which takes up exactly as though it's just another story in the series of 'epiphanies' of Art. The organic unity of the pair is demonstrated in other ways. *The Green Isle* is shot through with necessary memories of the first book, like Art's great race, or his wonderful knife, or the account of how he 'found' his ancestors 'under an Old Gooseberry Bush'. Most of all the link is in the river, with its fable of the salmon who eats the hazelnuts of knowledge to find wisdom. This was the burden of *Young Art's* very first story. Now, at last at the river, Art and Hector poke around a deep pool for salmon. Art climbs the hazel, gathering some nuts. Leaning over the pool, he falls in. Hector tries to rescue him, and they drown.

This typically arresting opening leads Gunn to his most daring fiction. It is a blend of folk-tale (the Green Isle is Tir-nan-Og, the

39

Celtic Paradise, in which Art and Hector find themselves), thriller-romance, and social satire in the anti-Utopian genre of *Brave New World, 1984*, and *Animal Farm*. Indeed, it has elements superior to these, since Gunn suggests that the positive life-virtues and community values of *Young Art* and all his Dunbeath experience can redeem the dystopia through the wisdom of myth.

The pair find paradise re-organised along rational lines of post-utilitarian sociology. Centres control rural regions; industrial peaks produce for the many; the fruit is processed, forbidden to the natives in its natural state. Watchers take strangers (presumably the newly dead) to the Questioners, who brainwash all primitive or anti-social elements out of their memories of the past. (One recalls that the opening of the novel showed the Highland community shocked not so much at physical atrocity as at mental.) To Gunn the spiritual essence, the soul, is the last atom of importance. Cancel that, and all existence is meaningless.

Art takes to his heels, becoming a legend, rumoured as older, mythical and magical descendant of the great heroes, attended by the great hounds of the Green Isle. Hector is captured and inter-rogated for long by the cool but ruthless psychologists who are fascinated by finding so much primitivism. Remember that this is a 'fable of freedom', presumably transpiring in the minds of the drowning Art and Hector. Such fables have their own rules, and within this framework Gunn is entirely consistent. Two ways re-main in the Green Isle to reach God. The first is through rumour (and thus through Art); the second is through the final right of any human being to ask to see God, which right Hector, at bay, finally asserts. It is superficial criticism to complain now of God's actual appearance; within fable and allegory the only right criticism is of how well the matter is handled. Gunn handles it marvellously. God is 'rescued' by the fleeing Art (note the daring of Gunn's sym-bolism) and turns out not only to look like old Hector, but to be almost certainly the Starter of the Great Race which Art won at Clachdrum in *Young Art*. The boy and the old man have reached the source of all Gunn's work, implied throughout: Love, Delight, Magic. The source turns out to bear a wonderful resemblance to the best things of the strath of their highland river.

Gunn was never to aim so high again. Effortlessly he resolves his fable by having Art and Hector rescued, with three strange relics —

the hazelnuts (of knowledge), the salmon (of wisdom), and the shared memory, private to themselves, of having glimpsed paradise and spoken with God.

Gunn now felt that certain central and mythical figures, especially those of Christ, Cain and Kronos, were locked in mortal combat in the post-war world. He now deliberately parodied certain kinds of novels, using their conventions in order to present a mythical answer. Thus the thrillers (*The Lost Chart*, *The Key of the Chest*, *Bloodhunt* and *The Shadow*), where the titles sound like those of Eric Ambler or Hammond Innes, but where Gunn's humour (Hart calls it 'transcendental comedy') puts in other meanings implying, in the first, the lost way of life of the Hebridean island for which the admiralty chart is the symbol. The key to a stolen seaman's chest is also the key to man's heart and its strange workings; in the drama of a policeman hunting the murderer of his brother there is the tracing back of killer and love instincts (Cain and Christ); and beyond the shadows round a cottage that has seen murder there is the shadow of modern totalitarianism and dogmatic socialism.

The closing three novels (*The Silver Bough*, *The Well at the World's End*, *The Other Landscape*) have this double reference, only with less of the thriller and more of self-mockery. All the protagonists are aging professional men — archaeologist, professor of history, and anthropologist. All get into long and sometimes grotesque conversations in weird places — hotel rooms with superbly cranky majors, caves with smuggler's stills, and the like. Deliberately, Gunn reduces the heroic in the action and emphasises the nonsensical and the farcical, although he also keeps a serious mythical strand running at their back. Here the quest for the Wordsworthian essence is taken as far as anyone has taken it, and with humour; but here also Gunn's metaphysical and aesthetic speculation becomes deeply complex.

In addition to his twenty novels, Gunn was an outstanding short story writer (*Hidden Doors*, 1929; *The White Hour*, 1950). He wrote several volumes of non-fiction, ranging from the subtle enquiry into the metaphysical 'spirit' of Scotland by way of examining the history of whisky, in *Whisky and Scotland* (1935) to the account of the 'great escape' of 1937, *Off in a Boat* (1938) to a series of cameos of the Highland year which set the values of the local and natural, the tiny but all-important details of life on this planet

41

against the dark backcloth of the war, *Highland Pack* (1949); and lastly but crucially, *The Atom of Delight* in 1956. He also wrote a tremendous number of articles for magazines like *Chambers Journal* and *The Scots Magazine* (which also contains a serial novel (1929–30) not afterwards published called *The Poaching at Grianan*); and he wrote plays.

All this was inspired by fidelity to and love of a traditional way of life, by 'staying at home', by being 'parochial'. In *Young Art and Old Hector*, Art asks Hector if he ever had gone away from his village:

'No,' answered old Hector. 'I often thought of going, but I never went.'

'Are you sorry you didn't go now?'

'No,' answered old Hector, 'Not now.'

His voice was quiet and Art looked up at him. 'How's that?'

'Well, if I had gone away, I wouldn't have been here walking with you, for one thing. And for another, I like to be here. You see, I know every corner of this land, every little burn and stream, and even the boulders in the stream. And I know the moors and every lochan on them. And I know the hills, and the passes, and the ruins, and I know of things that happened here on our land long long ago, and men who are long dead I knew, and women. I knew them all. They are a part of me. And more than that I can never know now.'

'That's a lot to know, isn't it? said Art wonderingly.

42

3 Lewis Grassic Gibbon: a Journey to Despair

James Leslie Mitchell was born in 1901 at Hillhead of Segget, Auchterless, Aberdeenshire, the <u>eighth</u> child of crofting parents. They moved to the Mearns in 1909. His parents appear to have been not so much unloving as unsympathetic to their sensitive boy, but what matters for our purposes is not the details of biography, but how Mitchell/Gibbon saw his biography. *The Thirteenth Disciple*, his second novel, is based on family experience, and the very title, implying both lack of luck and a sardonic reflection on Christianity, suggests Gibbon's way of seeing his development. Paradoxically, Gibbon was always proud of having been born a peasant even although so much of his work deplores the narrowness of the crofting people. The man who was to evoke the feel and smell of the farmed earth tells in his essay on 'The Land' how he conceived 'a very bitter detestation for all this life of the land and the folk upon it . . . in grey servitude to those rigs . . .'. Here is the root inconsistency, the first of many. He was an erratic and unreliable farm-worker, more interested in the marks of pre-history like flints and standing stones. As his essay on the future of exploration, *Hanno* (1928), shows us, this love of things past went with a far-ranging imagination of things future, an interest in the stars and their possible conquest. 'Of course I was thought to be crazy,' Gibbon told an interviewer in 1932. Already the two poles of time of *A Scots Quair*, time far past and time far future, were generating the metaphysical speculation of his fiction.

Such a childhood created a dual response to his parents and place. On one hand there is a frequent anger at father-figures like John Guthrie, authoritarian and unsympathetic to their children, and on the other, sympathy for 'my father's face, tired and sagging to weariness in the upspringing flameglow of a lighted lamp . . . ,' in *The Thirteenth Disciple*. Even as a successful writer his parents still thought him feckless and insubstantial. This can be seen in

43

Cloud Howe, when Chris and Cis Grant (in 'Nimbus') stop at 'a little farm high in the Reisk, over-topped by the wave of its three beech trees,' where they are given unstinting hospitality. This kindly picture is of Bloomfield and Gibbon's mother, who won't take money because her son was at college with Chris (true enough!). The other side comes in when she tells Chris that he now lives in London and writes 'horrible books'!

A pathetic picture of mutual misunderstanding emerges. Genuine parental concern and incomprehension caused dour, overstated, resistance. Each little mutiny or scandal made the next probable, such was the chain reaction of mixing such opposite natures and values. Ian Munro's biography skirts tactfully around the time of Gibbon's secondary schooling, leaving us confused about the role of Gibbon's primary schoolteacher, Alexander Gray, whose early help in writing and reading was obviously invaluable to Gibbon. We read that when Gibbon got into trouble at Mackie Academy in Stonehaven in a 'scene over a missing book,' or with the Rector (whom he pilloried as 'Sammy Dreep' in *The Thirteenth Disciple*), Gray was the mediator, always supportive of his star pupil. Munro reports how some accused Gray of being 'party to the youth's waywardness.' Was Gibbon spoiled by Gray, a surrogate son and proxy version of Gray's own literary dreams? Gray kept Gibbon's (and only Gibbon's) exercise books for over fifty years. One guesses at divided loyalties and wonders if here originated the 'two Chrisses' dichotomy Gibbon felt so deeply. In the boy's writing, too, a stilted, rather pedantic tone and phrasing, with condescension towards 'locals,' is found, as though for an approving and encouraging reader. Some of Ewan's priggishness in Grey Granite is here. In addition one wonders why Mitchell/Gibbon walked out of Mackie Academy; without disputing the authenticity of Munro's picture of the parental shame, and their pressure to 'get a fee' — that is, to become a hired farm labourer.

Gibbon at sixteen maintained his lonely defiance. He became a junior reporter with the *Aberdeen Journal*, and, 'adopted' by the Aberdeen family Macdonald, passed two of the happiest years of his life, 1917–19. A more comic division of loyalties occurred in this period when, as he tells us in the essay 'Aberdeen', he was sent to report on the founding of the Aberdeen Soviet, just as the news of the Bolshevik Revolution came through from Russia. He was elected to the Council, forgetting he was a press-man, which led to embarrassment later when explaining to his boss why as a good sovietist he couldn't report the meeting! This was the culmination of a development begun in schooldays when H.G. Wells filled him with visions of a World State and a universal language. This large-scale idealism never left him.

Whatever the zeal of his revolutionary politics (and he got into trouble with the police in these years because of it), ambition in letters took him to a well-paid junior reporter's job on the Glasgow-based *Scottish Farmer*. This spell in Glasgow, says Munro, made him aware of the class struggle, witnessing as he did Clydeside disturbances and industrial unrest. He joined a group with Communist sympathies (though significantly still seeing himself as 'one who in origins (peasant) was outside the war'). Munro also notes that 'he was strangely unaware of the character, humour, spirit and kindliness of the Glasgow folk' — an attitude which led directly to the anti-Glasgow diatribe in the essay 'Glasgow'. By now one detects what Munro calls 'a lack of stability' in Gibbon. How could one expect detached observation of the city whose newspaper now sacked him for fiddling expenses? Munro excuses the offence by arguing that Gibbon was only 18 and that many a young man has done the same. But the sum was half of a year's wages for Gibbon, £60, and obtained by ink-erasure of figures and substitution. In *The Thirteenth Disciple*, (to Gibbon's credit) no varnishing over the event is attempted, and it transpires that the motive was to gain money for revolutionary activities. If true, then Gibbon anticipated the 'end justifies the means' attitudes of Ewan in *Grey Granite*. It is one of the disturbing aspects of Gibbon's political thought that ultimately he backs any means to serve the Revolution's purpose.

It was at this time that Gibbon attempted suicide, and again, without petty curiosity, one would like to know more about this clumsy and, according to Munro, 'halfhearted' attempt. Was it a cry for understanding to parents who predictably failed to respond? Nervous breakdown now sent the boy home. Gibbon's return was bound to be impossible. Again, the demand that he get a fee. Again, the angry refusal. Note the paradox — that the celebrant of the freedom of Golden Age Man should now, in order to gain freedom, commit himself for all but the last five years of his life to service in Cairo and Mesopotamia and England in the very armed services he so despised, from August 1919 to August 1929. Typically he is contradictory in the way he expresses his feelings about these years. On one hand, he echoes T. E. Lawrence (of Arabia) and his grim statement in *The Mint*:

> We enlisted men have all been cowed . . . . Bitterly we know of experience that we are not as good as the men outside.

In *The Thirteenth Disciple* he describes in detail 'the festering moral reek of the barrack room', the debased sexual and social habits of servicemen, the dehumanising rituals of mindless drilling and medical inspections. One sees the origins of *Sunset Song's* bitter portrayal of the army's destruction of Ewan. On the other hand, he could melodramatise his situation in Egypt in letters home, so that (in classic foreign legion manner!) he becomes one of the 'children of the wanderlust', and is even boastful of belonging to 'the greatest fellowship of the earth':

> Right glad I am to be what I am without a future or a care for it, disreputable, a careless dreamer of dreams and a maker of songs that will never be sung, desiring what I have not, wanderer and vagrant predestined.

But upon return in 1923 from the first spell of service life with the R.A.S.C., Gibbon had little to hope for. Five months in London as down-and-out and sandwich-board-man must have showed him the face of despair and finally embittered him about 'the city experience' and the class struggle. In later and happier years in Welwyn Garden City, the pleasant garden city outside London where he made his final home, he pretended to newspapers and publishers that the five months had been far more romantic, and that he had managed 'to get a ship to Yucatan' where he roamed around studying ancient Mayan civilisation. The *New York Times* and other papers reported this lie, and it is in Ivor Brown's foreword to *Sunset Song*:

> . . . he told me, that he met an archaeologist who later took him to Central America, where he studied the remains of the Mayan civilisation . . . he attributed some of his subsequent

ill-health to that excursion; he told me once that his digestion had never recovered from the diet of maize on which he lived for some time amid the Maya ruins, following some years of a service diet.

This foreword also softens the sacking from the *Scottish Farmer* to 'falling ill' and coming home 'to help in the fields of the Mearns'.

I cite this material not to belittle Gibbon, whose humanity and courage I admire immensely, but to develop the picture of a highly complex and restlessly changing personality. Indeed, this very fallible but vivid sensibility is, I argue, what makes him a great writer, evoking as only he can Chris Guthrie's changing moods and values.

There is no doubt that in Mesopotamia, Palestine and Egypt he found the time-perspective which was to resolve the problem of his unhappy childhood background. His childhood love of the marks of pre-history in the Mearns was rekindled in visits to Alexandria, Cairo, the Pyramids, Bethlehem (spending Christmas Eve there!), and research work with a Cairo archaeologist; but more important was his developing vision of the "Cairo Dawn", or the beginnings of civilisation in Egypt and Mesopotamia. Here I suggest, lies Gibbon's basic strength and weakness, in that he now builds a 'philosophy' which is to permeate everything he will write; but builds it from the deeper and subconscious needs that he has to come to terms with his traumatic past. This young man sees family ties, values and community judgement as corrupt. He feels himself the 'outsider', the 'thirteenth disciple' and the martyr to false social values which depend on religious hypocrisy and an over-great respect for a 'speak' or gossip of community which sees success as material and the spiritual as crazy. Is it surprising that he should use all the evidence that suggests that the fault is not in himself but in the working of history? He has to show everyone being out of step but Gibbon: Civilisation wrong and Gibbon right. Having said this, what matters thereafter is not whether he's right or wrong, but how poetically and creatively he uses this idiosyncratic vision. Study of this reveals there are at least two Gibbons, if not more; that Diffusionism, the theory he adopted at this time, is far from being the whole story of his work, but that he was ultimately far too honest and courageous a man simply to be a fellow-traveller to such a convenient and self-justifying fable.

Neil Gunn, with his similarity of interest and vision first identified the deep basic split in Gibbon/Mitchell in an article in *The Scots Magazine* in 1938, called 'Nationalism in Writing: Tradition and Magic in the work of Lewis Grassic Gibbon'. This is a seminal piece of criticism in its awareness of the split between the creative artist and the concerned anthropologist haunted by the condition of the poor of the earth. Quoting 'the two Chrisses' passage of *Sunset Song* from 'Ploughing' where Chris feels the division between the side of her that loves the land, the folk and their Scots words and the English Chris who wants 'The English words so sharp and clean and true', Gunn argues:

> when Mitchell is using orthodox English he is manipulating intellectual rather than blood values, and consequently in the realm of the emotions such English does not move us with a sense of the unconditional magic of life or of that life's being rooted in the breeding soil of tradition.... Yet what a troubling division was in him just there!

For this orthodox English is part of the Wellsian Mitchell who saw (in his essays and political thought) nationalism as an obstacle to progress towards Cosmopolis, a state when slavery and physical want will have gone, and the 'Golden Age' returned, married to a new human maturity. Gunn suggests that the socially concerned Mitchell 'never imaginatively realised this Cosmopolis', but took it as inevitable 'not because of any ultimate need for it *in itself*, but because it was for humanity's final good *on the material or economic plane*'. Thus there is a Gibbon who *feels* and intuits rhythms and traditions and a poetry in man's relationship with the Land as a good *in itself* (the term 'magic' relates to this inexplicable connection) and a Mitchell who is social reformer, with a Diffusionist and revolutionary programme. Indeed in his Welwyn Garden City days this division manifested itself in some absurd ways, from references by Mitchell to Gibbon as 'my distant cousin' in essays (and vice versa) to different 'poses' for press interviews, two different signatures and even, Munro tells us, two different typewriters.

I now look at the short stories, essays and fiction other than *A Scots Quair*, but regard them in the light of this 'heart-head' division in Gibbon's mind. I suggest that within this division are the four positive 'creeds': Diffusionism, Communism, Christianity and 'Magic' — Gunn's term, which I will develop. Then I go further and suggest that one can put these 'positive', if often mutually inconsistent, reactions to life on one side, a positive side, of a split, the negative and dark side of which is a sardonic scepticism about all these shifts and dreams. Though fragmented, this is a very human and confused response to life, understandable in such a young man. Gibbon died at 34, and all his work (bar the extended essay *Hanno* (1928)) was published between September 1930 and November 1934 — four years covering an output of eleven novels, two books of short stories, three books of anthropology and exploration and (with MacDiarmid) a book of essays and short stories. (By contrast, Gunn's twenty novels, two books of short stories and four volumes of essay and autobiography are published over thirty years, 1926–56.) This is the intensity of a passionate young man, possibly aware of his shortness of time. Like Keats, in the hurried attempt to make sense of experience he resorts to some inconsistent solutions — with a despairing doubt that all of them are empty.

The solution Gibbon committed himself to most fully was Diffusionism. Some of his finest writing stems directly from it, but significantly this is to be found not in novels so much as essays like 'The Land' and 'The Antique Scene'. The most Diffusionist novels, *Three Go Back, The Lost Trumpet*, and *Gay Hunter* are (even to Douglas Young) his weakest and least imaginatively-convincing works. This isn't to say that Young is wrong in arguing that Diffusionism permeates all his work — it does — but where it is most successful, as in *Sunset Song* or *Spartacus*, it is a theory transmuted into a sub-stratum of haunting poetic idea, never, as in these propaganda-novels, clots of argument and lecture, or clumsy and improbable symbolic action. But in the essays Diffusionism can become poetry. 'The Antique Scene' is the base for study of Gibbon. Here is Gibbon's view of Scottish history, ending with 1745 and the last kick of the free folk of Scotland. Industrial revolution and modern Scottish social history are anathema to him, but he fills pre-history with poetic description, and sets forth a clear outline of Diffusionist belief:

All human civilisations originated in Ancient Egypt. Through the accident of time and chance and the cultivation of wild barley in the valley of the Nile there arose in a single spot the urge in men to upbuild for their economic salvation the great fabric of civilisation. Before the planning of that architecture enslaved the minds of men, man was a free and happy and undiseased animal wandering the world in the Golden Age of the poets (and reality) from the Shetlands to Tierra del Fuego. And from that central focal point in Ancient Egypt the first civilisers spread abroad the globe the beliefs and practices, the diggings and plantings and indignations and shadowy revilements of the archaic civilisation.

Then follow passages about how great bear and the red deer watched the arrival of the Golden Age hunters described by minister Colquohoun in *Sunset Song*, the Maglemosian and Cromagnard dark men: 'naked, cultureless, without religion or social organisation, shy hunters, courageous, happy, kindly...''. The archaic civilisation comes next to Scotland via the explorers and miners for copper and bronze of Crete and Spain. The simple hunters, welcoming them, 'set on their necks the yoke under which all mankind has since passed'. Now is the time of the building of the 'Devil Stones' by 'priestly overlords', with agriculture and 'the smoke of sacrifice at seedtime and harvest'. But the third and worst wave of 'civilisation' comes with the 'fringe-dwellers' of the great settlements, who are jealous of the 'improvements' and absorb only the worst of archaic practice. In this unusual view, the villains are the Kelts, far more villainous and savage than the wreckers of the Roman Empire, incapable of poetry, cultureless, merely a conquering military caste, and in Gibbon's view, the foundation of Scotland's landed gentry (as in his picture of Mowat the Laird in *Cloud Howe*). They rout the ancient sun-priests and bring devils and gods. Pytheas (whom Chris 'saw' in *Sunset Song*) sailed Scotland's coasts, by Gibbon's way of it, when they had just established their rule. But the Picts survived underneath.

The coming of the Angles and the Irish Scots ends serious colonisation. For us, the survival of the elder and good folk, the peasant Picts, is what matters, for they are Chris and Rob and Ewan and Kinraddie's best:

The Kelt, the Scot, the Norseman, the Norman were no more than small bands of raiders and robbers. The peasant at his immemorial toil would lift his eyes to see a new master installed at the broch, at the keep, at, later, the castle, and would shrug . . . turning, with the rain in his face, to the essentials of existence, his fields, his cattle, his woman.

Gibbon's typical and passionate praise of Wallace, Spartacus-minded warrior of the folk (symbol in *A Scots Quair* of what Ewan may do again, and better); his hatred of the way the nobles betray and cheat, and of the way the Church corrupts and of how the last elements of Commons revolt were crushed in the destruction of the Covenanters, clarify the Diffusionist interpretation of Scottish history:

> The Diffusionist school of historians holds that the state of barbarism is no half-way house of a progressive people towards full and complete civilisation; on the contrary, it marks a degeneration from an older civilisation. . . . The state of Scotland since the Union of the Crowns gives remarkable support to this view, though the savagery of large portions of the modern urbanised population had a fresh calamity — the industrial revolution — to father it.

Understanding this essay alone makes all Gibbon's work leap into relief. The haunting note of elegy which finishes it can be heard again and again in *Sunset Song*:

> . . . the ancient Pictish spirit remembered only at dim intervals, as in a nightmare, the cry of the wind in the hair of freemen in that ancient life of the Golden Age, the play of the same wind in the banners of Wallace when he marshalled his schiltrouns at Falkirk.

And the essay 'The Land' succeeds as literature precisely because Gibbon denies a factual approach:

> For if the land is the enumeration of figures and statistics of the yield of wheat in the Merse . . . I am quite lost.

51

He makes argument a fierce invective poetry, transforming himself from social theorist to passionate representative of the people, arguing and evoking what Spartacus and Chris Guthrie feel in their bones:

> I like to remember I am of peasant rearing and peasant stock . . . I feel of a strange and antique age in the company and converse of my adult peers — like an adult himself listening to the bright sayings and laughter of callow boys . . . while I, a good Venriconian Pict, harken from the shade of my sun circle and look away bored, in pride of possession at my terraced crops.

Already, amidst the poetry, are the inconsistencies. Gibbon boasts of a farming ancestry which makes him superior, when in *The Thirteenth Disciple* he called it 'a beastly life'. But, honest as Gibbon in the end always is, he admits the fact in the essay; 'for once I had a very bitter detestation for all this life of the land and the folk upon it. My view was that of my distant cousin, Mr Leslie Mitchell . . . .' Fair enough; but there's a deeper inconsistency yet, which is that Diffusionism argues that agriculture is the beginning of Man's Fall, of civilisation which is false. 'Man the free hunter' is Diffusionism's rallying call. But 'The Land' discovers that it is perhaps not the free hunter who is most memorable but rather that it is the very farmer whose agriculture, Gibbon frequently argues, was the beginning of man's slavery:

> This is our power, this the wonder of humankind, our one great victory . . . . Three million years hence our descendants out on some tremendous furrowing of the Galaxy, with the Great Bear yoked to the Plough . . . [the vision of *Hanno*] will remember this little planet, if at all, for the men who conquered the land and wrung sustenance from it . . . . Nothing else at all may endure in those overhuman memories; I do not think there is anything else I want to endure.

This was Gibbon's necessary and poetic vision. Where Diffusionism is a positively harmful influence is in the Mitchell novels like *Three Go Back* ('the least rewarding of Mitchell's novels' says

Young), *The Lost Trumpet*, and *Gay Hunter*. Douglas Young is excellent in his assessment of these novels, and I refer the reader to him (see the bibliography) and I draw attention only to certain aspects of these as illustrating my argument.

Three Go Back takes the boss of an armaments' firm, an American academic, and a best-selling woman novelist into the past — about 25000 BC — to lost Atlantis. The means of time travel is vague, but the point is clear — they are flawed representatives of modern civilised man, and they are to meet the Golden Age people. But as Young points out, Gibbon fails here (and in the other specifically Diffusionist novels) to 'realise imaginatively this strange new world'. (Compare this work with William Golding's evocation of states of mind and place of primitive man in *The Inheritors*.) Implausibilities abound. Golden Age primitives run as fast as wild ponies and mammoth; the American, Sinclair, knows the language of the Basques, and so do the primitive people; the novelist's lover, killed in the war, is recreated in the primitive, Aerte, who becomes her lover. Gibbon will use this device often, whereby Ewan will resemble ancient man, or (as in 'Forsaken') moderns will be reincarnations of past historic figures; but what's acceptable in a poetic and supernatural tale is not so in a Wellsian and scientifically-based argument. One particular inconsistency wrecks Gibbon's Diffusionism. He brings on a band of destructive Neanderthalers, impossible barbarians in a perfect world, since the corrupting events necessary to warp them haven't occurred. Thus the Gibbon Diffusionism crumbles and the needs of his plot and creative imagination imply, as Young says, 'that war and terror and suffering did exist in primitive times and that Sir John's [the militarist] view of primitive life was the correct one'.

Gay Hunter uses scientific romance similarly in its pictures of three characters going forward in time. This can be taken as a kind of sequel to *Grey Granite*, since it shows the kind of world which might have ensued ages after Ewan. Perhaps too it shows something of what went wrong with *Grey Granite*, since the two novels presumably share ideas uppermost in Gibbon's mind at the time. Is *Grey Granite* too close to scientific romance and the kind of these three Diffusionist propaganda novels, with their tendency to the improbable? *Gay Hunter* irritates with its time-travel, brought about by using J. W. Dunne's theory (in *An Experiment with Time*

1927) that one can, on the edge of sleep, will oneself into the future; especially when it's not just the heroine Gay who does this, but also the villain, a retired major, and Lady Jane, a bored aristocrat. They all project into the same place at the same incredibly far-off future time. Gay meets the requisite healing primitive, Rem — who can speak English! — and hears of the destruction of the old (our modern) world. Echoes of Wells's 'speaking history' in *The Time Machine* and of how society developed in *Brave New World* don't bring the book to life. And our time travellers hardly show the courage of their convictions in their pleasure at returning to what Diffusionism sees as our sick society.

The Lost Trumpet deals with the present with similar excessive Diffusionist argument and improbability of plot. The trumpet is no less than that which blew down the walls of Jericho, now hidden near Cairo. There is inconsistency in the symbolism, in that not only is there a magical provenance to the trumpet (prompting the obvious question — did it really work?) but also a Christian significance which co-exists awkwardly with the Diffusionist symbolism, that we must find this ancient life-giving music in order to discover our 'Golden Age' simplicity. The characters have modern 'walls' about them, walls of false 'culture', and walls of Calvinist repression and sexual fear. There are even actual castle walls imprisoning a princess walled in by the memory of a dead lover. Again, the symbolism is too heavy, allegory defeating actuality, and again implausibility reflects over-contrivance. The hero is the Conradian story-teller of *Calends of Cairo*, a white Russian professor of English and an army colonel now turned dragoman in Cairo. His English is laughably pidgin. Another of the protagonists is Aslaug Simonssen, an Edinburgh-Norwegian looking for the Cairo murderer of her brother, and the enunciator of Diffusionism is a gynaecologist (bringer to birth of new ideas!). Instability of vision and the need to make plot fit theory has brought about melodrama.

Diffusionism has its vital place in Gibbon's work; but in these formula tales the central failure lies in Gibbon's inability to make his Golden Age an imaginative reality. J. B. Priestley in a review and a letter (used in Munro's biography) puts the objections to Gibbon's 'Golden Age' arguments succinctly. He doubts, firstly,

54

the Rousseau doctrine of the noble innocent savage, the fair and frank child of Nature. I do not believe in him. He never existed and he never will. All this kind of sentimentality is as dangerous as any other, for our task now in this world is to make civilisation a great deal more civilised and not to abandon it in disgust.

And Priestley wickedly pushes home his point against all return-to-the-Land, 'Dark God', 'Golden Age' practitioners from Mary Webb to Lawrence to Gibbon when he adds, in answer to Gibbon's abusive complaint about his review of *Gay Hunter*:

> ... if you seriously think that primitive life was and is better than this 'of diseased abortions', then why live, with a telephone, in a Garden City, sign contracts in Great Russell Street, and employ the full resources of the Windmill Press? D. H. Lawrence tried to persuade us that life is at its best among Mexican Indians, but I was never able to understand why he troubled to write books ... when he could have thrown his typewriter away, taken his clothes off, let his hair grow, and become a Mexican Indian.

Slightly unfair, since Gibbon takes pain to stress that moderns can't go back, that it's the regaining of the good aspects of the Golden Age psychology that matters, but one sees the force of the attack. More important, Priestley strengthens his case by not dismissing the Golden Age totally as ideal:

> Nor has any anthropologist as such any right to tell me when the Golden Age was, or where, for every man has a right to discover — if he can — his own Golden Age.

This will be the greater strength of Gunn's position, that *his* concept of our buried subconscious ideal memory is realisable without throwing the baby of civilisation out with its dirty bathwater. Priestley's remark draws attention to another inconsistency in Gibbon's extolling of free man on the one hand and — especially in his later pictures of the ideal leader — a compulsory and end-justifying-means programme of destruction of civilisation. Clearly in *Grey Granite* or *Spartacus* there is little hope that the mass of the folk can achieve 'Freedom' through democratic self-improvement. They must be led to it, by cheating and guile if necessary.

His other 'creed of the head', of social reform, was his communism, although he was always sceptical about commitment to any one creed. Storman the communist is satirised in *Stained Radiance*; while Ewan and Trease in *Grey Granite* are out to use the movement as means to anarchistic ends. Gibbon's friends seemed confused as to his allegiance, James Barke saying that he was a clear communist before his death, MacDiarmid claiming that he had become an out-and-out Scottish Republican. What is in no doubt is that he cared passionately about a revolution in the state of the world's poor; and that, like Malcom Maudsley in *The Thirteenth Disciple*, he could rage at political movements and wash his hands of his commitment to them because of their sloth or tendency to pointless dream. The essay 'Glasgow', in its picture of the speakers on Glasgow Green, shows this, with only the communist speaker (with no audience) allowed dignified comment. All others, from Guy Aldred's Non-Parliamentary Anarcho-Communism to Orthodox Socialism ('ruddy and plump, with the spoils from the latest Glasgow Corporation swindle in its pocket'), Fascism, and Social Credit (MacDiarmid's enthusiasm, but to Gibbon 'that ingenious scheme for childbirth without pain and — even more intriguing — without a child'), being impatiently dismissed as evading the commitment to revolution.

In espousing Diffusionism Gibbon found a detached answer to a personal psychological need that removed tension and guilt. With his politics, instead of writing to formula he writes to powerful, sometimes uncontrollable feelings — so that where we found the mainly Diffusionist novels flat and ratiocinative, the political essays and novels are flawed because the emotion cannot be controlled. 'Glasgow' has great strengths, but its most vivid and feeling passages are its weakest, intellectually and argumentatively. Gunn cites Gibbon's welcoming of a 'Chinese army of occupation' as demonstrably irrelevant to the problems of Scottish economy, far less the problems of the hundred-and-fifty-thousand of the slums of Glasgow whose plight Gibbon feels so deeply. The hysteria comes in as his rage mounts and finds no immediate outlet: For example, on 'Scottish Culture' which he hears 'ad nauseam':

the patter is as intimate on my tongue as on theirs. And relevant to the fate and being of those hundred-and-fifty thousand it is not more than the chatter and scratch of a band of apes, seated in a pit on a midden of corpses.

Presumably then the song-culture and beautiful poetry he shows and employs at Chris's wedding in *Sunset Song* is also as irrelevant, and his discussion of culture in 'Literary Lights'. But of course in different mood Gibbon would not argue thus. Or again, on small nations, in the same essay; an interesting example, since (like so much of the anecdotes of horror in his work) it comes in (and by his own explicit admission!) as irrelevant. Glasgow, he says, provides him with the excuse to splurge on 'small nations'.

> What a curse to the earth are small nations! Latvia, Lithuania, Poland, Finland, San Salvador... the Irish Free State... an appalling number of disgusting little stretches of the globe claimed, occupied and infected by groupings of babbling little morons... mangy little curs a-yap above their minute hoardings of shrivelled bones.

In this mood police are seen as 'rat-brained clowns' (*The Thirteenth Disciple*), servicemen 'atavistic little perverts', scholars 'apeptic pedants in the British Museum Reading Room' whom he wishes he had 'at bayonet practice'! 'Clownish' becomes the adjective for anything from the Norsemen to the councillors of *Grey Granite*, till one sees that at worst in his politically impatient mood the entire world is 'clownish' and insufferable to him. Whenever political argument enters Gibbon's fiction, unless it is treated with irony (as with Chae's socialism or Rob's reading of Ingersoll, the 'watchmaker' in *Sunset Song*, as Fascism and nationalism and socialism in *Cloud Howe*), it just doesn't work. The satire at Ramsay MacDonald's expense in *Cloud Howe* is wisely and successfully not given the same kind of treatment as in 'The Wrecker', that fierce attacking essay. And *The Thirteenth Disciple*, the Mitchell novel with the greatest amount of political (and autobiographical) involvement, functions as a novel more successfully because the pseudo-editor looks at Malcom Maudsley's political career with a certain ironic mockery. Nevertheless, it is worth looking at

Malcom's programme of reform since it obviously shows Gibbon's sympathies, and shows how impossible it would be for him to find a single label for them. Since Malcom can't find socialism or communism to his entire taste, he forms his own 'Secular Control Group' — and this is its programme:

SOCIAL AND POLITICAL: (i) Abolition of the Legal Status of Marriage. (ii) State Propaganda and Enforcement of Birth Control. (iii) A General Tax to be levied for the Endowment of Each Woman's First Two Children. (iv) Complete Secularisation of Education. (v) Disestablishment of Churches. (vi) Repeal of the Blasphemy Laws and Censorships.

INDUSTRIAL: (vii) Nationalisation of Banks. (viii) State to Acquire Controlling Shares of Principal Industries.

SCIENTIFIC: (ix) Compulsory Periodical Dissolution and Reorganisation of all Chartered Learned Societies. (x) State to Acquire all Patents and establish a Department for the endowment of *Bona Fide* individual Research.

ANTI-WAR: (xi) International Organisation of Associations pledged to both Passive Resistance and Sabotage.

One sees the difficulty in making poetry of such matter, and the danger of loss of control, because the issues do matter so much.

At first sight it appears redundant to examine Gibbon's religious beliefs, since as Diffusionist and revolutionary he abandons them on principle. But Christianity played two vital roles in his work. First, as in James Joyce's 'damned Jesuit strain', as provider of imagery and poetry from a field in which Gibbon grew up, so that his work is littered with reference to the Bible and Christian lore, and he uses the image of Christ's crucifixion alongside the image of the trapped and maimed soldier on barbed wire as his two images of man's horrific inhumanity to man. And secondly, even more inconsistently, as *belief*; with a commitment to love and respect and recognition of the supernatural hand of Christ in action.

The first aspect is easily and quickly proven from a reading of his work from the early poetry ('Dust'; 'I see the Christ, an outcast, stand forlorn/A dream, a tale, a wonderment of tears') to 'Greenden' and 'Forsaken'. The first tale uses the song of Calvary, 'There is a Green Hill', as ambiguous but possibly satirical indication that the girl who sacrifices her reason and her life for her husband's health has done so on account of an unhealthy dream. The second brings Christ himself to Duncairn (city of *Grey Granite*) to find his former disciples become realists and communists who forsake him. It should be noticed though that the story presents a further problem — for it argues the *existence* of Christ, *and* the supernatural reincarnation of his former allies. It's a realistic fable, with kitchen-sink surroundings and industrial unrest, and its implication is clear: that Christ is or was Good incarnate, but that so fallen is this world that his dream will no longer be achieved by his methods.

It is important to see that Christ was to Gibbon the outstanding martyr, chief of a line from Spartacus to Wallace and, in *Sunset Song* and *Cloud Howe*, Long Rob and Robert Colquohoun. It's even more important to realise that at times Gibbon used Christ and Christian imagery as meaningful background. Consider 'For Ten's Sake' (1929). We meet, on Easter Day, an old geologist obsessed with ideas of revenge on the murderers of his son in Mevr, 'Hell-Gate of the East', city of prostitutes and thieves, at the crossroads of the Asian caravans. 'How long, O Lord' he cries. He ignores pleas for help from those of the city whose destruction he craves. Gibbon vividly paints the degradation, and foetid heat and the old man's delight when he realises that earthquake will destroy the city shortly. But amidst his mad delight, in the street of Ten, the foulest of places in Mevr, a phrase increasingly haunts him. In his mind (like the 'strange words not her own' which Chris is compelled to utter at the end of *Cloud Howe*) 'an unknown voice' starts counting the episodes of courage which occur as the earthquake begins. The words are those of the Bible:

> Peradventure there be fifty righteous men within the city. Wilt thou also destroy and not spare the place for the fifty? ... ' ... And He said, I will not destroy it for ten's sake'.

The old man collapses, his son's killers save him, and he learns his son to have been wicked. Desperately he counts, and finds nine righteous men; then at the eleventh hour, he finds his tenth, a shadow in the corner beyond the thieves and murderers:

he saw stand for a moment One whom he had never known,
One with bleeding hands and feet and hidden face.

The vision of Christ crucified brings the old man's redemption,
physical and spiritual — and the corrupt humanity of Mevr is saved.

'And the Cock Crew' depends on its characters' identification
with St Peter, Simon and Judas, and *Spartacus* ends with Kleon's
vision of the crucified Christ (together with Spartacus) triumphantly prefigured in the heavens. How could Kleon the Greek, dying
crucified a hundred years before Christ, know of Calvary? *Cloud
Howe* also uses vital Christianity at its point of deepest vision.

What this shows is not just inconsistent with the 'scientist's' Diffusionist diagnosis and the communist cure; it shows us Gibbon's
need for emotionally and aesthetically satisfying myth and poetry,
not to be found in the conclusions of the head, but in the quests of
the heart. Indeed, beyond Christianity one sees Gibbon's quest for
tradition and magic, a clearly recognisable fourth strand. Time and
again, Gibbon's tales rely on magic to achieve their deepest effects.
Statements in the novels as where characters like Long Rob or Chae
imply total rejection of religious thinking, can blind us to the fact
that he *says* many a thing, but *does* many another. The view of his
essay 'Religion' sees all religion as 'a cortical abortion' performed
on naturally Good but Godless man. Gibbon wants release from
religion to

a strange and terrible and lovely world, the world of science
and scepticism and high belief and free valour — emerging
into the sunlight of history from a ghoul haunted canyon.

Why then in 'Daybreak' does the meaning lie in the magic? The
Scottish heroine, with the symbolic name of Dawn, is dying in
Egypt at the end. At the eleventh hour, the wind changes into the
Delta wind, 'a green wind'. It brings even to the narrator who has
never been in Scotland, the never-before-experienced smell of
heather — with objective corroboration from Dawn's husband. 'My
God! he whispered. 'Did you smell it? *It was heather*!'. And the
narrator *sees* the purple slopes of a Scottish valley. Under enough
emotional stress, Gibbon will always bring in magic. *The Thir-*

teenth Disciple gives Malcom his death-vision of the Golden City of the Mayas, and of human hope, just as on the other side of the world his wife gives birth to a son. Kleon sees Christ at the end of *Spartacus*. In *A Scots Quair*, in the first two novels, Chris, Chae, Guthrie, Robert and John Muir are given supernatural vision.

Gibbon needed such episodes to achieve a deeper purpose than that which Diffusionism or reason could provide. This is exactly the 'tradition and magic' which Gunn so admired in his work, and lies behind *Stained Radiance, The Thirteenth Disciple* and *Image and Superscription*, much finer novels than the Diffusionist-dominated three. They anticipate the themes and situations of his best work, although it's obvious in the changes of style, narrator and tone (from irony to lyric enthusiasm) that Gibbon is still searching for a coherent voice. In each there is a character or characters who stand very close to Mitchell's own history and attitude, tormented by a warping religious background and enthused by Diffusionism — but not to the point of being taken over by it. Rather, these Gibbon-surrogates follow and hunger for a dream, a vision of something beyond Golden Age man or theory. For example, Malcom Maudsley all his life has explored 'beyond the Walls' even from his first pages of experience, when we see him as a sobbing child clutching a stone with which to shatter the horizon. Found at night, weary and dirty amidst the moors, 'the stone was still clutched to his chest and the conviction firm in his heart that beyond the next scaur, the next stretch of gorse, an incredible adventure awaited him'. Malcom's beginning prefigures his end. He dies in Yucatan pursuing the Golden City of this dream of magic. (Ironically, the real Maya city of the ancients he seeks is the flower of a cannibal and clever civilisation.)

More important than Diffusionism, the idea of quest dominates these novels, and the quest is for adventure, magic and love, in terms that are religious rather than scientific. In 'Daybreak', Roger Mantell speaks for a part of Gibbon when he finds an 'other thing':

> . . . has led us up through the dark Defile of history, has turned in many guises to help again and again the stragglers and the lost in their hour of utmost despair. It will lead us to the sunrise yet.

61

We are close to the split heart of Gibbon's complex and fragmented vision. Time and again when he seems to have closed the door on all metaphysical discussion of God he reopens it by suggesting the existence of such a force. Probably no more confusing term than 'God' is used in Gibbon's work, since he uses it to denote the false dreams Man must fight, as in Ewan's and Chris's war of Freedom against God, described by Ewan in the closing pages of *Grey Granite*, or in a totally different sense in the closing pages of *Spartacus*, when the Gladiator-leader, rising to heights of greatness and love for his fellow-slaves, finds 'a God' within him. In this second sense we are using the term as 'Daybreak's mysterious force which isn't either the theology of a Robert Colquohoun or the Godlessness of Chris Guthrie, but the force which drives a Ewan or Malcom or Spartacus.

How then can I argue that Gibbon moves towards a 'dark vision' or despair? In *The Thirteenth Disciple* Domina Riddoch, the Diffusionist heroine, speaks for Gibbon when she whispers yearningly, 'I'm God's man, Malcom, if you can find him for me'. Like Domina, Gibbon is bleakly honest. I think that beyond the four positive if confused responses lies an opposing and sardonic scepticism. Against the dogmatic and loving Seeker-warrior is placed the Doubter, who questions every dream. The moment of realisation comes in reading 'The Land'; when the full depth of Gibbon's horror of existence suddenly reveals itself. Celebrating the end of winter and the release of the cattle from the byres, vividly he conveys their delight, humorously he describes their grumphing and galumphing and racing around and happy mooing, their racing a grocer's cart the length of the field. Then, with no warning:

> they abandoned playfulness and took to grazing, remembering their mission was to provide fat carcasses for the slaughtershed.

It is not the cows who remember, but Gibbon, who continues:

> We balk from such notions, in Spring especially, in especial as the evening comes with that fresh smell all about it, impregnating it, the kind of evening that has growth and youngness and kindliness in its essence — balk from the

thought of our strange unthinking cruelties, the underpit of blood and suffering and intolerable horror on which the most innocent of us build our lives. I feel this evening that never again will I eat a dead animal... the Horror is beyond personalism, very old and strange and terrible. Even those (Golden) hunters all those millenia ago were eaters of flesh.

Over-sensitive, raw-skinned, agonised — but honest in its dismissal of his favourite dream. Typically inconsistent, he shortly revokes this view by saying that dogs tortured, horses broken, rats tormented with red hot pokers in bothies disgust him, but 'do not move me too deeply, not as the fate of the old time Cameronian prisoners... in Dunnottar... not as the crucifixion of the Spartacist slaves...'.

But the glimpse has been enough. One knows now that Gibbon has at bottom a horror of the meaningless cruelty of existence. Critics reproved his indulgence in scenes of sadism and violence, from the recurrent image in the fiction of the man on the barbed wire to the castrated victim of civilisation, from the tortures of the Mayas in his study of their civilisation to the scenes of agony in the cellars of Dunnottar castle, from the agony of dying horses in *A Scots Quair* to the agony of dying Romans and slaves in *Spartacus*. There is a long drawn-out cry of horror and agony in Gibbon's work. I suggest though that what this reveals is not self-indulgence in sado-masochistic fantasy so much as a horrified fascination which draws him back again and again — not to the horror for its own sake, but to the possibility that it may be the random, pointless norm of a pointless universe. Behind Gibbon's portrayal of such scenes lies the pain of wondering why? Why can this happen? In the face of this all his other creeds seem lesser ideas.

And the Horror need not be physical violence or pain. More frequent are the endless moments of doubt, when Malcolm or Kleon or Rob Galt's daughter in 'Clay' wonder about the reason for human endeavour.

Thus in the end there are two poles. There are confused 'head-heart' credos, often at odds with each other, and there is agonised or ironic scepticism. The real creative tension lies between these two poles and produces his finest work. This story and that novel often reflect but a side of Gibbon. But there *was* development, a movement to a voice which could objectify these warrings. He had some reason in the invention of the pseudo-editors of *The Thirteenth Disciple*, *Image* and *Superscription*, or the narrator of the early Cairo stories. They were ways of not taking himself too seriously, of sliding out of the accusation that he was his protagonists. They showed most of all the need for distance and detachment, which Gibbon found for *Spartacus*, the Scottish short stories, and most of *A Scots Quair*. The detachment is necessary, for finally the vision in fact is ambivalent, arguably reversible. I suggest that his greatest work successfully embodies a dual vision, a presentation of the riddle of existence which permits a response of hope or despair.

Consider 'Clay', the story of Rob Galt, a decent Mearns crofter. The story is told by 'the speak', and much of *Sunset Song* is here in embryo — the father's servitude to the land, his daughter Rachel's wish to go to college, the hardship of the mother, the place of the croft and its people in history. But Galt is no Guthrie, loved as he is by Rachel, and 'a fine, frank childe . . . kindness itself'. Rob has asserted his independence by breaking from being foreman with his father and buying the croft of Pittaulds (the name suggesting ancient Pictish agriculture). But a 'queer-like' change comes over him and Galt becomes short-tempered to his family and obsessive about his farm work. Cleverly Gibbon transposes the language of sexual and family love from Galt's relations with his family to his relations with the land — fields are 'woman you'd to prig and pat afore they'd come on', or 'bitches', or 'on the sulk', and he caresses the soil, running it through his fingers. He's not cruel like Guthrie, but his wife, now terminally ill, and daughter, disappointed in her hopes of college because of his greed for the land, now mean hardly anything to him. The story can be read so far as Galt's pursuit of an obsession. But what comes in now is eerie and deliberately open to supernatural interpretation. Galt begins to take in moorland, 'wild and unfed since the Flood', as locals tell him. But Rob sees it otherwise; 'Maybe, but they're queer-like, those braes, as though some childe had shored them tight up.'

In heaving out a great root (the roots of his race) he finds an earth-house, with the bones of a man of the antique time, and his flints and implements for tilling the soil. Rob also finds his own death. Hauntingly suggested is the notion that with Rob's vision of his ancestors a wheel has come full circle. Rob has linked up with his ancestors, and something great is completed. Unlike the ending of 'The Land', there is no explicit praise or blame for the generations who farmed, but an open question, asked by Rachel before she goes to a life away from the land:

> And she thought of the men who had made these rigs and the windy days of their toil and years . . . was it good, was it bad? What power had that been that woke once on this brae and was gone at last from the parks of Pittaulds?

Douglas Young argues that the story ends 'on a note of optimism' — 'Rob may be destroyed but the next generation — represented by his daughter Rachel — will yet return to nature, to a more true and ancient way of life.' But Rachel does not, and the rhythms of the close suggest, as in Chris Guthrie's end, a rule of Time and Earth in which man has little place, since whins and broom, wild, manless growths, triumph, and humanity are Earth's 'hungry bairns in her hungry breast where sleep and death are one'. But the story permits of levels of interpretation: Galt as a warped good man and farming as corrupting; or Galt as somehow noble with an ancient dream, fulfilled at the cost of family, but disturbingly epic; or finally Galt and farming as an intrusion on a Nature which does not need humanity.

'Smeddum' seems at first uncomplicated humour, with its 'earth-mother' Meg Menzies as a force of nature, uncomplicated in her independence and vigour. But there are deeper considerations. Meg *is* the Land, resilient as nature itself. Her children (nine) 'couldn't but live' given her scruff-of-the-neck shaking to life — 'Day blinked and Meg did the same' — together. But, like Chris in relation to her son Ewan, she is the Past to her daughter Kathie, trapped in her obligations and the land for all she talks of Smeddum and freedom. Thus Kathie is, in a way Meg herself; but going on to be the new age, like Ewan, enriched by identity with the past, but accepting no necessary obligation to it.

Lack of this saving sense of self is the theme of 'Greenden', the most difficult of Gibbon's stories. Douglas Young's interpretation is admirable, arguing that the story has levels of interpretation. This first is that it is a story of self-sacrifice, with the wife Ellen Simpson re-enacting Christ's sacrifice. Gibbon's skill in weaving the hymn together with the actual green hills of the Cairngorms which Ellen sees through her restricting trees is masterly, as is his ability to suggest that we may need to reverse the parable and see her sacrifice as unnecessary, as 'the distortion of Innocence by Civilisation' as Young puts it. Her husband survives in the rank growth of modern farming and the gossiping Murdochs, growing, vampire-like, 'thicker and bigger' where she is 'thinner... more of a wisp than ever', till her lonely spark of sensitivity is quenched by Murdoch's building his new barn across her life-line view of the hills. Gibbon keeps his distance through the folk-narrator, so that no single message comes through. The suffocating woods, with their beast-like presence, become in one sense the projection of Ellen's sense of malice and beast-like gossip about her. Her enigmatic 'God died, but I needn't, He saved him, not I' can be taken as not merely the ramblings of a crazed woman, but a dim realisation that she must not follow her Christian sense of duty to a self-destructive conclusion. I think in the end, though, that the tale is confused, because Gibbon puts one further and disruptive element into his story. The den is haunted by a padding beast which even Grocer Webster senses, a presence which is not merely Ellen's projection, but the ghost of the former owner, Old Grant, whispering yet in the uncanny stillness of the breathless and unclean place. Even the narrator feels the trees threatening and the broom whispering and the 'beast with quiet breath'. And so another reading can see an ancient evil breathing through the den woods. 'Greenden', then, is powerful — but confused, since the opposing views damage each other.

At the back of the tale is a sense of waste, of human effort unavailing in the face of the Horror as in the last of these Mearns tales, 'Sim'. Sim Wilson has only enough vision to go from one shallow dream to another, Golden Age man gone wrong in a world which can give him none of the rewards of the ancient life. His repeated cry is the cry of sceptical Gibbon: 'show me a thing that is worth my chave and I'll work you all off the face of the earth!'. The valid object is never shown — unlike Rob Galt, Sim is not even given a private view.

Gibbon's great achievement of these last years was *Spartacus*. Here, all his elements are richly interwoven. The Diffusionist background is subdued and ironically presented. A burning but controlled political anger makes the novel an allegory on modern inhumanity, while there is a living use of Christian symbol and the figure of Christ, with a sense of man's traditional quest for a magical and transforming vision of life. But there is more; for so distanced is Gibbon from his creation that the sardonic and doubting vision is there too, in Kleon, the Greek intellectual, a permanent reminder of 'the Horror' with his castrated body and warped, coldly-amused mind.

If *Sunset Song* has its 'speak', *Spartacus* has its terse, detached almost inhuman narrator, who has seen legends born and die; who, the sardonic rhythm and tone implies, has no illusions left. The single outstanding feature of a protagonist becomes his dry motif: Kleon, 'to whom life was a game'; Castus, 'who loved Spartacus'; Gershom ben Samballat, 'who loathed Gentiles'; Titus, always madly remembering the 'Men of the Western World', or Brennus and his brother, longing to hear the lowing of the aurochs, the wild ox of their lost homeland, ancient Gaul. The violence and cruelty, abundant and sickening, comes over with a dry understatement which convinces us that indeed life was thought to be cheap. As nowhere else except in *Sunset Song* and 'Clay' there is a wild and magnificent poetry of image, and legendary moments which combine to create, as only Gibbon and Gunn can do, the sense of *myth*. Unforgettable is the scene where Spartacus, maddened and bewildered from a head wound, addresses the temperamental gladiators he has led in escape from Rome:

> 'I remember hunting wolves', he put up his hand to his head, 'long ago. When the packs were about us in the wintertime I and the others kept in a band and reached home in safety. We neither stayed among the wolves nor scattered and ran —' He stopped, staring, a troubled, tremendous figure to the eyes of the slaves; and then sat down. Elpinice stood up, her woman's voice strange and mild in the bass rumblings of the ragged horde. 'The Wolf is Rome. Spartacus will lead us from Italy, but only as a united army. Let us march and meet the next army of the praetor's.'

This captures perfectly the notion of an event in history, awkward, accidentally successful and destined to become legend and myth. The same is true of Spartacus with the great white stallion which is his prize from the beaten legion of Furius:

> All stared, Spartacus now silent, with strange, glazed look and heaving breast. Then they turned their gaze to the giant stallion which stood shivering beside him. Its nostrils were still in the grasp of his great fingers, and as the general of the strange host groaned, his knuckles whitened and the stallion groaned beside him.... Those near at hand cried out to Spartacus to beware, but he did not move, staring at the stallion. It heaved its head and snorted with quivering nostrils between its knees till its white knees were spattered with a bloody foam. Then it raised its head and slowly, hesitatingly, made a step towards the Gladiator.
> The leader of the slave-horde had found a mount.

The power of this has nothing to do with argument and political belief. It is a mythic poetry which Gibbon recurrently achieves, the highest point for me being the terrified and awe-struck vision which the Roman legions have of Spartacus when they have been pursuing his army up to the Italian Alps. Against the advice of lieutenants, Spartacus stays behind, alone in the mist to brood over his slave-horde who have become part of himself. The lower legions stumble through the mist. Then, the mist clearing, they stand aghast at the figure helmeted in gold, 'armoured, immense in the spreading glow of the mist, the sun suddenly upon him. So he gleamed like a God, and the legions stared and murmured...'

Spartacus was written just before *Grey Granite*, and to my mind is the successful version of what Gibbon tried unsuccessfully to do with Ewan and his workers in the unconvincing beginnings of revolt in Duncairn. Partly the success here is due to the fable-form, the actions of the century before Christ not calling for the kind of persuasive social verisimilitude that the modern novel requires. But in part the success is due to the skill in staging Spartacus's development, and also to the fact that of all Gibbon's novels this is the quest-novel which finds Love — not sexual or the personal emotion of lovers, though that is here — but love as empathy and identification with humanity. Here the cry of horror merges with the agony of love, as Spartacus *becomes* the slave-horde, just as Ewan becomes suffering poverty, but with a strange poetry and lonely dignity which Ewan never attains. This is due to the presence in Gibbon's mind of Christ, with whom Spartacus will be merged in the final cosmic vision. Ewan's heartless treatment of Ellen Johns is not Spartacus's way with Elpinice or the slave-girls who willingly serve him. Ewan's priggish coolness has no counterpart in the Gladiator and most important of all, Ewan's belief that the end justifies the means has no place in Spartacus's conduct, who turns time and again from success because he feels the rightness of giving immediate aid, even to those who, like Gannicus and Castus, betray him. He abandons Rome not on his own account, but for his men. He finally destroys himself because there are no more ends more important than dying with his men.

But lest all this suggest a novel of unmitigated affirmation of Christ's endless fight, Gibbon has continually opposed Spartacus with Kleon. By the same method as he uses in *A Scots Quair* he gets over his old problem of being too much himself in his heroes by creating characters who represent a side of himself. Gibbon dramatises the conflict within himself. Kleon represents that side in Gibbon which saw life in *Cloud Howe* as a 'midgeswarm', a game, or worse, a malignant horror. Kleon's maimed body causes him to retreat into cold aridity of intellectual theory and his playing with Platonic theory of a Republic is Gibbon's way of being ironic about political theorising. Kleon is the head to Spartacus's heart, and, in contrast to *A Scots Quair*, we are led to believe that the heart eventually wins this struggle since cold Kleon is warmed despite himself through anger and pain to the point where he transcends his limitations of feeling, covering the retreat of the slave-horde and expecting to die in so doing. Kleon, who started by amusing himself with the idea of playing Spartacus like a puppet in a game of chess with Home, ends by dreaming of a 'Lex Servorum', a new and better age. Spartacus continually makes inroads on his inhumanity by dismissing his Platonic Republic since it too has slaves, and by introducing him to new human experience. The miracle is achieved, whereby Kleon moves from arguing:

'What does it matter one way or the other, when all we do or dream are but blowings of dust' to seeing, before he dies on the cross:

> before him, gigantic, filling the sky, a great Cross with a
> figure that was crowned with thorns; and behind it, sky-
> towering as well, gladius in hand, his hand on the edge of the
> morning behind that cross, the figure of a Gladiator. And he
> saw that these Two were One, and the world yet theirs; and
> he went into unending night and left them that shining
> earth.

So why then call this chapter 'a road to despair'? I think that
Gibbon had temporarily in this novel reasserted the dominance of
his Christian vision, with Spartacus finding 'a God in men'. Let us
be clear of the limits of this vision, however. Christ is an ideal expression of an endless fight — but the God behind him, as Spartacus says, is 'an unknown God'. What *has* sustained this novel
more than religious vision or liberal humanism or simple vision of
endless revolutionary struggle is Love. And, as I will show, as Gibbon follows his road in *A Scots Quair* the vision of Love seems to me
to give way to a vision of Time, Change and negation — the Horror
in the end.

4 *A Scots Quair: Sunset Song* and the Song of Death

'The Floo'rs o' the Forest' was Jean Elliot's eighteenth-century lament for the Scottish dead of peasantry and nobility who perished at the battle of Flodden in 1513. It was the Sunset Song of the Golden Age of Scottish Culture, which under James IV — also killed at Flodden — had produced peace, poetry and a stability for Scotland all too rare, and not to be seen again for three hundred years. It is also the song behind all Gibbon's *A Scots Quair*. It is sung by the heroine, Chris Guthrie, at her wedding; it is piped as the lament at the end for her friends and her husband who died in the war of 1914–18; and it is the 'Song' given as title for the whole of *Sunset Song*, as well as being symbol of the death of song throughout the trilogy.

A Scots Quair is about the death of song and community in the small crofting community of Kinraddie in the Mearns, the land between the Cairngorm mountains and the North Sea, and how the community loses its ancient way of life which its songs, its stories, its way of speaking and its traditions express.

Part of the greatness of Gibbon's achievement is the depiction of the harsher side of peasant life and farming community, and another part is his sad vision of mankind having lost its way, of having betrayed itself by imposing false Gods in place of what Gibbon saw as the cleanness of sun and hunting in the dawn of time. One can question Gibbon's rightness of vision, question whether he was right to see primitive man as superior in culture and habits to modern civilised man, and one can question his accuracy of drawing in his picture of country life. Many have, and fairly. But no one has questioned the skill and power of his third great achievement in *A Scots Quair*, his story of the growth of Chris Guthrie, the central figure in the trilogy. No one has better captured the divided loyalties of youth, Chris hating and loving her background at once, or the tensions of adolescent womanhood. Gibbon's achievement is seen as all the greater when, at a point somewhere through the second novel, *Cloud Howe*, we realise that she is not only Chris Guthrie, but 'Chris Caledonia', the nation Scotland, married to the land in the first novel of the trilogy, producing her peasant son of strength for the future in Ewan. In her marriage to the church and Robert Colquohoun in the second novel, Chris produces a short-lived child as Gibbon saw it, the result of Scotland's relationship with the church. Finally, Chris marries the joiner, Ake Ogilvie, and is placed in the city. *A Scots Quair* moves from village to small town to metropolis in each of its parts, mirroring phases of Scottish social history as Gibbon saw them; and Scotland-in-Chris is shown as finding no fulfilment in her relationships with religion, industrialisation and urbanisation.

The quality of individual character and community life are adversely affected by the movement from local identity to urban impersonality, and *Grey Granite* shows us the wasteful process in its terminal stages. Therefore, its characters have little of *Sunset Song*'s invigorating comedy and tradition to relieve their plight. I think that *Grey Granite* expresses very powerfully what Gibbon wants it to express, although it's not so entertaining or moving a picture as *Sunset Song*.

Taken as a whole, as one great novel with three massive movements, *A Scots Quair* is a powerful statement about waste, loss of tradition, and social deterioration in the modern world, and I do not fully agree with the criticism which finds only *Sunset Song* totally satisfactory, with progressive 'falling way' in *Cloud Howe* and *Grey Granite*.

Nevertheless, only *Sunset Song* can stand clear of the rest of *A Scots Quair*, enabling us to read it as the separate epic of the end of an old community song. Even then it shows — for a complete novel on its own — loose ends, like the introduction of such a strong character as Robert Colquohoun, or the unanswered questions of Chris and Ewan's destinies. Obviously its plan leaves these connections open for *Cloud Howe* to make, and *Cloud Howe* has reference to the past, in its Kinraddie memories, and the future, in its introduction of characters like policeman Sim Leslie and Ake Ogilvie who suggest further development. *Grey Granite* is most ghost-haunted of all, with Long Rob, Robert, Chris's dead child, and the Standing Stones of Kinraddie or Kaimes Castle all functioning as part of Gibbon's dark vision only if they are living memories in the reader's imagination from the previous parts.

Taken together, these two points determine my treatment of *A Scots Quair*, especially if we accept that *Sunset Song* will inevitably be the most frequently read part of *A Scots Quair*. Allowing that *Sunset Song* can be read in isolation, and that it is the most popular part, I propose to study it in some depth in the first half of this chapter. Then I will consider *Cloud Howe* and *Grey Granite* as parts, ensuing and developing movements making up *A Scots Quair*.

Let us go back to the title, *Sunset Song*. Consider the implications of coming darkness and dying music, with echoes from Scottish history such as Chancellor Seafield in his 1707 epitaph for lost Scottish nationhood terming the end of Scottish Parliament 'the end of an auld sang'. The theme of death, with its attendant emphases in the novel of man's treatment of his fellow-men, on the shortness of life and the transience of pleasure and song is dominant throughout *A Scots Quair*, even allowing that at times there are moments of joy or apparent signs of hope expressed through Ewan and his communist beliefs. Chris's song dominates the trilogy, lamenting not only the death of Kinraddie's 'flowers of the forest', but also Scotland's loss of hero-martyrs throughout the ages from Calgacus to Wallace and the Covenanters.

However, images of Sunset and Song are images of beauty and life also. Light may go, but sun shall return. This double-sided, ambivalent statement of Gibbon's is what makes *A Scots Quair* difficult to read clearly. It is both negative and positive. And beyond the Sunset and the Song there is another major and ambiguous image. The Standing Stones, these remains of the first priests and farmers who settled in Scotland in pre-history, are the spine of the novel. Chris is found beside them in each chapter, seeking refuge and peace. They seem timeless and comforting in a world of impermanence and change. Yet they are also 'memorials of a dream long lost' and signs of 'ancient rites of blood and atonement'; that is, symbols of cruelty and death.

Thus I stress at the outset Gibbon's dualism; his mutually opposed attitudes within his *A Scots Quair*. Mitchell/Gibbon remained confused and unsure about his feelings for parents, community and farming in the Mearns. The escape to Mesopotamia and finally to Welwyn Garden City was purely physical, since (like the Irish writer Joyce, who 'escaped' the nets of 'nationality, language and religion') he found that the main content of his best work was bound up in Scottish nationality, language, and religion. This showed itself in a peculiar mixture of love and hate for the Mearns and its people, which in turn was written into Chris Guthrie's feelings and dreams.

Upon this tension between positive, diffusionist and communist Gibbon and negative, death-and-change Gibbon *Sunset Song* and the entire *A Scots Quair* finally depends. Thus Gibbon's dual vision, his 'love-hate' for his background and the Land, leads to a split pattern; 'Love' set against 'Hate' (see opposite).

I realise that in sketching the pattern of the novel thus I am artificially separating aspects which should be taken together. But I maintain that the two contradictory voices of Gibbon nevertheless underlie all the book's many changes of mood and tone, and that to separate the two extremes in the end helps us to understand that this novel is not about realities of the north-east farming situation at all, but about a deeply disturbed and dying man's responses to it. It is his unique vision of it. Kinraddie — and Segget, and even more Duncairn — exists in Gibbon's vision, and even then in contrasting sunshine and darkness.

The motion of Harvest illustrates Gibbon's double-edged symbolism well. In the 'positive' reading of the book it is the idea of fruition, birth, and fulfilment which shows itself both in the recurrent harvests of Kinraddie (mirrored in the chapter-heading, all stages in the rhythmic progression to it, from 'unfurrowed field' to 'ploughing', 'drilling', 'seedtime' and 'harvest' itself), and Chris Guthrie's own harvest, her child Ewan. But there is a 'negative' parallel to this reading, in that it is the men of Kinraddie who are 'harvested' by the Great War. Gibbon intends that much of his symbolism should ask us the question — is nature more a process of wastage and squandering of life, than one of renewal and birth?

Let us look at the hopeful indication, the affirmative themes. On the 'love' side of the novel, Gibbon conveys to us a vivid and detailed celebration of the vigour and humour of north-east life. Mainly this achievement is dependent on 'the speak', that voice of the collective community, the 'stream of consciousness' of Kinrad-

74

LOVE	HATE
a positive statement of themes, such as:	a negative statement of themes, such as:
the celebration and lyrical evocation of the rhythms of the Land, and the good-humoured, if satiric, picture of its people (via the 'speak')	the presentation of Kinraddie (and its 'speak') as increasingly debased, with local and national institutions like the church and government seen as making martyrs of community heroes from Wallace to Long Rob; an increasingly mechanised society
the portrayal of the strengths and virtues inherited by the modern descendants of the 'elder people', Guthrie, Rob, Chae, Ewan and Chris; the memory of the 'Golden Age'	an underlying vision of waste and horror socially triumphant, and an increasing preoccupation with man's cruelty and violence to man and the 'martyrdom' of the good; the black harvest of 1914–18
the enthusiastic presentation of their irreverence and defiance of 'authority' and repressive power, religious or capitalist	a constant reference to man's tendency to illusion and dream
all particularly seen in in the *active* Chris, who accepts bond with Earth and has her own harvest in Ewan, her son.	all seen in the *passive* Chris whose dreams are taken from her, who loses Ewan, her husband, and who is moving towards recognition of two entities only, change and death.

die. This, in method, was one of Gibbon's two great innovations in Scottish fiction (the other being his unique and rhythmic prose style). 'The speak' can express a sense of warm community:

> And faith! broke he might be but he wasn't mean, Chae, when the folk came trampling in to eat there was broth and beef and chicken and oatcakes . . . and if any soul were that gutsy he wanted more he could hold to the turnip field, said Chae . . . .

> Maggie Jean . . . Gordon she was, none the better for that it might be, but a blithe little thing, thin body and bonny brown hair, straight to walk and straight to look, and you liked the laugh of her . . . .

> And you minded Long Rob right well, the long rangy childe, with his twinkling eyes and his great bit mouser and those stories of his that he'd deave you with, horses and horses, damn't! he had horses on the brain . . . but for all that he'd been a fine stock, had Rob, you minded him singing out there in the morning.

As in *The Silver Darlings*, this community creates its bonds and affections. Memories of a good wedding, a fine girl, a man's courage, his love of animals and his songs are held and passed on by 'the speak'.

The 'speak' changes its tune all the time, moving from grudging praise to outright condemnation. Consider the passage in 'The Un-furrowed Field', when, representing the common man or woman through the ages, it refers to Laird Kenneth the Jacobin, advocate of the French Revolution's programme of 'liberty, equality, fraternity'. Kenneth sells off property for 'the cause':

> More than half the estate had gone in this driblet and that while the cripple read his coarse French books; but nobody guessed that till he died and then his widow, poor woman, found herself own no more than the land that lay between the coarse hills, the Grampians, and the farms that stood out by the Bridge End . . . . some twenty to thirty holdings in all,

the crofters dour folk of the old Pict stock, they had no history, common folk, and ill reared their biggins.... The leases were one-year, two-year, you worked from the blink of day you were breeked to the flicker of the night they shrouded you, and the dirt of gentry sat up and ate up your rents but you were as good as they were.

The sympathy given to the Laird (just before this 'he had a real good heart') and lady, and the hostility to the crofters ('common folk') is almost simultaneously retracted, and the 'speak' quite suddenly and moodily changes tone and identifies with the very folk it attacked, now asserting its own worth stridently. Here is the fickleness of Shakespeare's mob! But it *can* praise and enrich also, although this kindlier voice is less and less heard throughout the novel and the trilogy.

There is also 'allocated' speak — that is, a similar method of oral comment, but the speaker identified. Most important as wholesome and sardonically corrective voice is the running motif of 'and Long Rob said':

> And Long Rob of the Mill would say what Scotland wanted was a return of the Druids, but that was just a speak of his, for they must have been awful ignorant folk, not canny....
> But Rob said he'd rather be a thorn than a sucker any day, for he didn't believe in ministers or kirks...Rob said...if Christ came down to Kinraddie he'd be welcome enough to a bit of meal or milk at the Mill, but damn the thing he'd get at the Manse....
> And Long Rob said...*the more education the more of sense and the less of kirks and ministers.*

He is the good-humoured voice of common-sense, debunking and correcting the stupidity of Kinraddie. Gibbon uses him throughout as foil to folly.

The 'speak' and the speech of the novel can be at once derogatory and somehow celebratory in the sense that we both laugh at the scathing comment and enjoy its vigour and energy. Oddly enough, Gibbon's book implies an attack on gossip the same way that *The House with the Green Shutters* did, but relies on the gossip and the anecdote to enrich itself. Without the 'speak' and the gossip *Sunset Song* would be a thin chronicle indeed. And in quality of metaphor which is the staple of the novel *Sunset Song* stands above *Cloud Howe* and *Gray Granite*, for it uses rich organic and animal metaphor to describe situations and local worthies:

Farmer Munro— 'a creature from down south . . . a good six feet in height, but awful coarse among the legs, like a lamb with water on the brain';

His wife — 'a thin creature, with black snapping eyes like a futret', who on hearing gossip 'reddened up like a stalk of rhubarb in a dung patch';

daft Andie — 'a meikle slummock of a creature, and his mouth was aye open, and he dribbled like a teething foal.'

Tony is 'a gowk', and almost everybody in *Sunset Song* is likened at some point to animals like sows, weasels and foxes. As Long Rob said, the majority of folk were either sheep or swine, Chae being an exception, since he's a goat. One of Kinraddie's lairds is carted off, crazy, crying 'Cockledoodledoo'; the next is 'as proud as a cock on a midden'; Mistress Gordon 'was a muckle sow of a woman' 'with eyes like the eyes of a fish, fair cod-like', with 'only a dove's flitting of a family'. In evoking the feel and smell of the earth and the sweat and struggle of farming, Gibbon's only equals are Hardy and Lawrence. This is Gibbon's 'Song of the Earth', in which sunset is a part of rhythmic rebirth and decay, part of a cycle of nature.

Once again, Long Rob emerges as a key figure, as the main 'singer' of the song. Like Gunn, Gibbon sees 'Song' as the comprehensive symbol for living tradition, a 'music' or socially harmonious force generated by the community for the community, enriching and enshrining its most precious values and remembrances:

They'd hear Rob out in that coarse ground hard at work when they went to bed, the rest of Kinraddie, whistling away to himself . . . *Ladies of Spain* and *There was a young maiden* and *The Lass that Made the Bed to Me*.

Rob is always singing defiantly against Kinraddie's growing snobbish hypocrisy and new-fangled sexual coyness. His singing of 'Bonny Wee thing, Canty wee thing' saves Maggie Jean Gordon from being raped by Daft Andy, who, on hearing it, changes from ravening beast to gentle simpleton, singing the song himself as he puts Maggie Jean on her way. Similarly Rob's singing pulls Chris back from the horror she feels when her own father, afflicted by that strange 'harvest madness', lusts after her. Elsewhere Rob's singing is described (like Gunn's symbolism in his novel *The Lost Glen*) as 'an echo from far in the years at the mouth of a long lost Glen'. Rob, back from jail as a conscientious objector, sings his old songs to young Ewan. The 'lost glen' image denotes Rob's place as one of the old singers of an ancient culture, now losing itself amidst modern change. It is Rob and Chae who supply music, fiddle and melodeon for Chris's wedding. And although the wedding songs turn to sadness in the end, their importance as songs of the earth, 'made for the sadness of the land and sky in dark autumn evenings', cannot be overstressed. It is the song of blood and life that Chris, above all, feels; 'as though her blood ran so clear and with such as fine sweet song in her veins'.

The clearest and strongest theme of affirmation, and probably the theme most close to Gibbon's creative heart, is that of the 'Golden Age' and the survival into the present of descendants of the 'Elder People'. Their connection with the land is ancient:

> It wasn't bad land, the Knapp, there was the sweat of two thousand years in it, and the meikle park behind the biggings was black loam, not the red clay that sub-soiled most of Kinraddie.

When Chris watches Ewan and Rob ploughing together,

> she heard Ewan call *Ay, man, Rob* and Rob call *Ay, man, Ewan*, and they called the truth, they seemed fine men both against the horizon of Spring, their feet laired deep in the wet clay ground, brown and great, with their feet on the earth and the sky that waited behind.

Land, and men who work on it, are being sung, praised, in such lyrical descriptions.

Gibbon slowly develops the idea of a long line of descent through two thousand and more years from the 'Elder People' to the circle of friends and relatives in Kinraddie (but not all of Kinraddie by any means) who are 'the last of the peasants', as Robert Colquohoun describes the four killed in the war. Thus a group made up of Guthries, Chae, Rob and Ewan contrast in their values with the changed and debased attitudes to the land of the Mutches and the Munros, who go in for mechanised and battery farming, who have no 'feel' for the land (witness their stripping of the sheltering woods of Kinraddie for quick profit) and who belong firmly to subsidy-farming as a business concern rather than to farming as a way of life.

The 'Elder People' stand for two broad groups of ideas. On one hand, they are the last of the ancient hunter-farmers who remember the free days when church and state did not exist. Rob and Chae and Chris are instinctively hostile to class snobbery, the dictates of ministers and the law and politics of the nation, for these are unreal to their concerns with the land as something felt in the blood. On the other, this deep racial or tribal memory, similar to Gunn's 'collective unconscious' in *The Silver Darlings*, has built up over centuries a community feeling where loyalties don't depend on cash transactions (witness the way the members of the group immediately help each other at fires, or harvests, or bereavements). Traditional festivals, the calendar of events in the natural year, the loving raising of crops and children and animals, a love for organic and growing things, are portrayed by Gibbon as being the characteristics of the 'Elder People' of modern Kinraddie.

One might feel that John Guthrie, with his bigotry and cruelty, hardly fits in such company. But despite these adverse features he has a core of integrity which we should admire. If we remember his deep personal loyalty to friends, his love of animals, and his total refusal to give way before pompous snobbery, we find a stern, hard man who stands on his own feet and fears no one. He is first introduced to us with his golden-haired wife, having won the ploughing match, carrying off woman and prizes like one of the Corn kings of old. But, as Chris is to realise, 'God had beaten him in the end' — which is a strange but true way of telling us that Guthrie is a good man warped by his excessive Calvinism. When Guthrie went up to the Standing Stones, to get Chris:

he glanced with a louring eye at the Standing Stones, and then Chris had thought a foolish thing, that he kind of shivered, as though he were feared, him that was feared of nothing dead or alive, gentry or common . . . he stood looking at the stones a minute and said they were coarse, foul things, the folk that raised them were burning in hell.

Why would he shiver, unless the Stones somehow affected him? If he despises them, they should simply be dead idols, not the only things we see in his life to frighten him. They reach him because they speak directly to him, and Gibbon means us to make the link between them and him, to realise that he is after all one of the ancient people, kin to those who raised these Stones. But his religion won't let him practise birth-control, so his wife dies. It says not to take the name of God in vain, so Will is whipped for saying 'Jehovah'. It represses natural instincts and a free delight in things sexual, so he disapproves of Chris doing the washing in her knickers. Yet when all nature seems ripe and even, his repressed desires creep out towards his daughter — this is expressed in the 'caged beast' metaphor applied to him. A fine man in tune with much that is good in nature, at harvest 'he grew stronger . . . ripe and strong with the strength of the corn'. He too is associated with Song — but, since religion has taken him over:

> hymns, these were the only things that he ever sang, singing with a queer, keen shrillness that brought the sweat in the palms of your hands.

His wife is an older Chris, who tramped the land barefooted, literally feeling the land through her limbs:

> She'd never forget the singing of the winds in those fields . . . or the daft crying of the lambs she herded of the feel of the earth beneath her toes. *Oh, Chris my lass, there are better things than your 'own' books or studies or loving or bedding, there's the countryside your own, you its.*

She has all the easy naturalness Guthrie lacks, as she laughs at his neurotic narrowmindedness.

There is no doubt that the theme of 'last of the peasants' can be taken at a concrete historical level, in the sense that the day of the small farmer is over. But Gibbon means us to look at these farmers more deeply, beyond the level on which we see them move to the small towns of Scotland and thence to the industrial centre. Ewan thus takes on a connection with the land that is uncanny. He is 'an awful good worker, folk said he could smell the weather and had fair the land in his bones'. He is likened throughout to a sleek animal a simple, cat-like, instinctive person, with a blood-knowledge of the land:

> ploughing his first rig, bent over the shafts, one foot in the drill, one the rig side . . . cleaving the red-black clay. The earth would back like a ribbon and curved and lay; and the cloud of gulls cawed and screamed and pecked on the rig and followed . . . . All over Kinraddie there were horse-pairs out, though none so early as Ewan's.

Ewan is the simple peasant. He doesn't share Chris's interest in folk history, and fails to see that it's *his* folk who were martyred at Dunnottar castle. His world has become the Land, Chris and his son to come, 'his gaze far off, and dark and intent', the crops and the earth in his bones and blood. It is the outside world of states and politics that destroys Ewan but it is his return to sanity and his ancient identity which leads to his death in a world which has no place for anachronisms like 'the Elder People'. His desertion from the trenches is meant to be seen as heroic — and tragic. He tells Chae:

> *It was that wind that came with the sun, I minded Blawearie, I seemed to waken up smelling that smell . . . . Mind the smell of dung in the parks on an April morning, Chae? And the peewits . . . and the singing there was, Chae?*

Ewan's last moments are with Chae, his 'brother' in peasantry. Two episodes clearly link Chae with the 'Elder People'. Home on leave, he cries out in anger when he sees that the long wood above his farm has been cut down. It has been a profitable exercise for Kinraddie, the woodmen paying high for their board, but Chae sees that the cutting of all Kinraddie's woods is the end of Kinraddie's fertility. But before he dies he is given a strange experience. In the moonlight where standing stones used to be, he sees 'a carter billy' kneeling. Suddenly there's no carter, only the crying peewits, and Chae realises that the helmeted man 'maybe . . . was one of the men of old time that he saw there, a Calgacus' man from the Graupius battle when they fought the Roman'.

In the same way Finn of *The Silver Darlings* or Kenn of *Highland River* were flashed backwards thousands of years when they entered the ancient Druid places. Symbolically, Gibbon uses this kind of incident to show us the modern descendant of the old earth people, as in the short story with so much of the essence of *Sunset Song*, 'Clay'.

If the trilogy had simply celebrated the Land and its continuity, Long Rob would naturally have emerged as Chris's next husband and mate, fitting partner from the Land, rather than as her doomed lover. His comments are a sort of moral back-bone behind the moving values of the 'speak', and he more than anyone *is* the Song of the Earth. Like Roddie, the 'Viking' of *The Silver Darlings*, Rob is the Viking figure here, always associated with horses, which he insists on using despite the coming of the tractor. He refuses to follow anyone's Gods or political beliefs, even Chae's. He only half jokes when he says he would like the return of the Druids. Rob endures any degradation that the modern state through police or army can inflict upon him. He is Spartacus or Wallace, with the crucial difference that he has lost the urge to start a rebellion. Finally he goes to war because, like Chae, he knows that the life of the Land as they knew it is ended. 'It's finished, Chris quean', he says, anticipating her words at the end of *Cloud Howe*.

Chris is the heart of this group, the essence of Kinraddie. But which Chris?

> So that was Chris and her reading and schooling, two Chrisses there were that fought for her heart and tormented her. You hated the land and the coarse speak of the folk and learning was brave and fine one day, and the next you'd waken with the peewits crying across the hills, deep and deep, crying in the heart of you and the smell of the earth in your face, almost you'd cry for that, the beauty of it and the sweetness of the Scottish land and skies . . . you wanted the Scots words

83

to tell to your heart . . . and the next minute that passed from you, you were English.

Is Gibbon here speaking for himself and a much deeper personal division than would be probable for Chris at the time of her development in the novel? I admit the rightness of the kind of division in Chris, but think that Gibbon superimposes his own feelings on top of hers, as the unusual use of 'you', not frequently deployed on Chris's behalf betrays. Here is the start of the Chris/Ewan fluctuations of spiritual identification which pull *Grey Granite* apart.

For the moment however we are concentrating on Gibbon's success in creating a Chris who is actively a part of the 'Elder People'. The other Chrisses belong to our examination of his dark vision; they evolve towards a cold understanding of death and change.

'The Unfurrowed Field' makes the briefest mention of the Guthries, reminding us that they are incomers, anticipating the day when once again it will be without them. Nevertheless we can see that the title of the chapter has related to Chris, in that she too is 'unfurrowed', inexperienced in life. Certainly she is so when we first meet her at the beginning of the first part of the novel proper, the novel proper being called *The Song*, and the chapter 'Ploughing', yet again validating the 'Song of the Earth' fusion. This is the beginning of the song that is Chris's life, the song that will reveal itself to be 'The Floo'rs o' the Forest'. Clearly Gibbon relates her to the June moors, the broom, the Land, reinforcing this design by introducing her in this context at the outset of each following chapter. We meet the Chris of school-learning almost immediately also, to let us know of the competing factors in her life. As with her father and with Chae, a peculiar incident reminds us that beneath the veneer of books and ambition to leave Kinraddie lies one of the Elder People. For it is given to Chris to see in vision or waking dream the coming of Pytheas, the Greek traveller, symbolising to Gibbon the coming of the first great barbarism to Druid and Pictish Scotland. Thus it is the ending of the 'Golden Age' that Chris witnesses in her seeing of the half-naked, black-bearded Greek who announces the ships of his master. Such vision is only given to the descendants of the Elder People. But what causes Chris to mature most in this part of her life is the death of her mother, which is recalled at the beginning of 'Drilling':

. . . it scored her mind as a long drill scores the crumbling sods of a brown, still May.

She is the 'May', the maid who encounters the tinker and then the kiss of Ewan, who awakens her femininity. This, with the departure of her brother Will to the Argentine, finishes her adolescence — 'the ploughing was done, she was set to her drilling'. 'Seedtime' sees her again seeking and finding comfort at her standing stones, again recalling what's gone before: the death of her father, and her own marriage and seedtime. This is the high point of Chris as an active, affirmative, happy person in tune with the Land in the rhythms of her own body, delighted at kindness shown at her wedding, singing the traditional songs. She does indeed lose the private Chris Guthrie, but in her place is the burgeoning Chris Tavendale of the end of this chapter, whose 'dreams were fulfilled', 'in her body the seed of that pleasure she had sown with Ewan'. This chapter sums up the Chris of the Earth. We will never again meet her so content and at one with it:

> . . . for this was her rig and furrow, she had brought him the unsown field and the tending and reaping was hers . . . sleepless in the long, dark hours for the fruitage of love that the sower slept all unaware, they [mothers-to-be] were the plants that stood dark and quiet in the night.

Six years are allowed to pass before 'Harvest'. This is important, since it tells us that the simple bearing of Ewan is not to be the only or the most important harvest Chris gathers in. What then is this more important harvest she has to find?

Once again we come back to Long Rob as a key figure. He has resisted all attempts to force him into what he sees as a crazy war. Ewan is dead in France, although Chris does not yet know this. She will have another of her uncanny experiences in which he returns (like Tormad to Catrine in *The Silver Darlings*) to make his peace with her. Put crudely, she betrays Ewan and makes love during harvest with Long Rob. But to read the episode like this is to fail to see that far from being a fall on Chris's part, it is the culmination and highest point of her relationship with the land. Chris, hurt by Ewan, turns to her Mother the Earth, to labour in the fields:

For she sank herself in that ... the way to forget, she was hardly indoors from dawn to dusk .... Corn and the shining hollow stalks of the straw, they wove a pattern about her life ... she turned to the land, close to it and the smell of it, kind and kind it was, it didn't rise up and torment your heart, you could keep at peace with the land.

Into this organic peace comes Rob. From realising that she had not known him, beyond being the cheerful miller, 'now it seemed she had known him always, closely and queerly'. She *has*; because Rob is her male counterpart, the mate she might have had, the greatest of the Elder People yet remaining, the voice of Kinraddie's Song. What then happens is almost predestined:

And she never knew when and how in the days that followed, it came on her silently, secretly, out of the earth itself, may be the knowledge she was Rob's to do with as he willed, she willed ... a man to love her, not such a boy as the Ewan that had been.

Their union is the height of Gibbon's lyric description of the rhythms of the earth. He sets their love in the background of a long harvest, on a land almost animate and breathing, so that their act is natural, clean, and part of the ultimate rhythm of nature:

Rob was there, and she drew his head to her breast, lying so with him, seeing out below the rounded breasts of the haystacks the dusky red of the harvest night, this harvest gathered to herself at last, reaped and garnered and hers in her heart and body.

Although Rob then goes, never to be seen by her again, this is the fulfilment of the Chris of the Land. Rob will be remembered as far on as the closing pages of *Grey Granite* but never at length, always in an understated reflection of Chris's, so quietly thought and expressed by Gibbon that the sensitive reader knows that so much more lies behind the brief mention.

Chris, then, is the female, and Rob the male, centre of the Elder People. This Chris is *active* in her life, making her choice in marriage, deciding, against her relatives' wishes, to stay on at the croft when her father dies, responding fiercely to social injustice — as at Dunnottar castle, when 'hatred of rulers and gentry' was 'a flame in her heart'. She has celebrated her womanhood, and Gibbon has shown her harvest. It remains for him to complete the picture of his Elder People by forging his symbolism completely. How better than to carve their names in memorial on Chris's and their standing stones to remind us that time has come full circle, that they are the last of the men of that kind? Robert's sermon makes it clear, together with the playing of their and Chris's Song, 'The Floo'rs o' the Forest', that they *were* the Land, the old speech, the old songs. Robert also makes the affirmative plea that their memory should be used to counter the evil of the machine, of new oppression, and finishes *Sunset Song* with the hope that they and the Elder People will not have existed in vain.

In this reading the novel ends with the image, not of the gathering darkness in which Chris and Robert stand by the memorial of the Stone, but with the image of regeneration of Robert's 'greater hope and a newer world', and lit by the Morning Star of his text from the Book of Revelation, with its promise, and its claim that 'even now' Rob and Ewan and Chae and James Leslie and Will, Chris's brother, her mother and John Guthrie still cry their answer to a modern, machine-dominated world's tormented questions.

I now take issue with Douglas Young and his argument that Gibbon/Mitchell 'is always a writer with faith . . . the sun which sets will rise again; a new golden age will come again'. It all depends on which Gibbon one listens to, and increasingly in *Sunset Song* and *A Scots Quair* it seems to me that the negative voice is heard.

As the old songs die out in Kinraddie, Chris reflects that their place has been taken by '*Tipperary* and squalling English things, like the squeak of a rat that is bedded in syrup'. And the 'speak' voice of the novel corroborates this:

> You heard feint the meikle of those old songs now, they were daft and old-fashioned, there were fine new ones in their place, right from America, folk said, and all about the queer blue babies that were born there, they were clever brutes, the Americans.

87

The rat image will come to dominate *Cloud Howe*; and the implication that it is humanity that is trapped, squeaking and brutalised with it. Kinraddie loses its Song, and Gibbon sees little in it to redeem the loss. The loss must be seen as occurring in two stages: over more than a thousand years; and from the beginning of the latest nightmare, the outbreak of war in 1914, which very quickly overwhelms the remaining community identity of Kinraddie.

This ties in with Gibbon's Diffusionist beliefs. How does 'the Unfurrowed Field' present Scottish history? In sweeping terms, as 'unfurrowed' — that is, untouched and unspoiled — until the Picts and their horses of the Aberlemno Meikle Stane were imposed on by barbarians. The Picts and their horses, like Rob and his horses, give way to a 'tormented place', haunted by beasts such as gryphons which exist only in tormented minds, like the later many-headed beast of Gossip which comes to roost in Kinraddie (like the beast in the story of Kinraddie's dark places, 'Greenden'). Cospatric gains land and authority by 'killing' it (with the implication that his entire authority, as of all those who follow, is falsely derived). But paradoxically it is to survive as cruelty, rumour and malice. What better image as emblem for the stories of betrayal, horrific cruelty, and injustice which follow? Hereafter, whenever such mythical beasts appear, they develop the theme of the corruption of the natural in man. Chris Guthrie laughs at the pretentiousness of her Anglified teachers in Duncairn; and we find the badge of the school carved on the main building — 'the head of a beast like a calf with colic . . . whatever the brute might be doing there'. Again, when Chris explores Edzell castle and its 'heraldic beasts without number', 'she knew right well that such beasts had never been, but . . . she grew chill where the long grasses stood in the sun, the dead garden about them with its dead stone beasts of an ill-stomached fancy'.

These beasts of mens' minds are to be contrasted with *Sunset Song's* presentation of natural animal life: Rob's hardy but healthy relationship with his horses, the love of the Guthries for their Clydes and Nells and Besses. Increasingly throughout the trilogy, man's relations with animals is one of exploitative cruelty (witness two examples in *Cloud Howe*: the death of Old Jim and

Dite Peat's killing of the pig); or man dispenses with animals in favour of tractors and reapers, only keeping battery chicken farming, or sheep. Alongside this run images of increasing mechanisation. Horse-drawn carts give way to bicycles and farm machinery; whenever motor cars appear, with their anonymous lights sweeping through a wondering village, they do so with harm to the community. They cost Guthrie his Donside farm, they take away Rob, and bring him back ruined; in *Cloud Howe* they bring home the Fascist Laird, and lorries remove Chris from Blawearie. It is for the making of aeroplanes that the woods of Kinraddie are cut down: 'The woodmen... left a country that looked as though it had been shelled by a German army,' thinks Chris — and the point is that to Gibbon what has come about *is* as bad as invasion, that Kinraddie and Scotland's home-inflicted wounds are every bit as harmful as anything going on beyond the hills.

By 1911 Kinraddie is a shell, like Barbie in *The House with the Green Shutters*, deriving little leadership from its bankrupt, inbred gentry. Already incomers, like Ellison, Munro and the Sinclairs, are taking over. There's no minister and the parish lacks fertility in land and children. Instead its 'dafties', Tony and Andy, are sneered at like the figures of Faith, Hope, and Charity in the church. A voice of hate sniggers and sneers with filthy suggestions as to why folk have had to marry, or where they got their money from. This voice reduces everything: an ordinary person to a 'coorse tink brute', a blushing face's being 'raddled... like the leg of a tubercular rabbit when you skinned the beast'. This voice calls a smile a 'daft-like simper', the choir of the church 'the calfie's stall', and loves suggestions such as that Chae started the fire in his own farm. This voice is that of the Kinraddie beast of Gossip, the prevailing voice of what becomes a wasteland.

The notion of 'wasteland' has a particularly strong appeal to the Scottish writer. Writers like Muir, MacDiarmid, Gunn, Mitchison and present day writers like Crichton Smith and Mackay Brown use the idea as a pattern for re-discovery of social purpose and value. Muir moves through his wasteland to put one foot, at least, back in Eden; MacDiarmid in *A Drunk Man Looks at the Thistle* took his thoughtful drunken Scot from a vision of the thistle as sterile rubbish in arid Scottish desert to fruitful and gestative silence; Gunn brought the wasteland to life again through his Fisher-kings, Roddie and Finn; and today in novels like *Consider the Lilies* and *Greenvoe*, Crichton Smith and Mackay Brown envisage regeneration through a similar pattern. Gibbon too works with such a pattern, with an awareness of ritual and symbol, from his presentation of Guthrie and his wife as a northern Corn king and Spring queen to his description so often of Kinraddie in wasteland terms:

> ... all the parks were parched, sucked dry, the red clay soil of Kinraddie gaping open for the rain that seemed never-coming... the hayfield was all a crackling dryness and in the potato park... the shaws drooped red and rusty already. Folk said there hadn't been such a drought since eighty-three.

This description opens Part One of 'The Song', 'Ploughing'. But in each part thereafter, through extreme damp or dryness, Kinraddie suffers a wasting of its earth — with two exceptions, when Chris's mother dies and when Chris works at harvest with Long Rob. The unnatural weather is the accompaniment for Kinraddie's unnatural attitudes. One remembers the way the unnatural heat accompanied Daft Andy's sexual rampage and Kinraddie's horrified delight in the stories of it, with Munro's sadistic assault on the simpleton; or the stifling heat surrounding John Guthrie's toad-like lustings for his daughter at harvest time, or 'the red, evil weather' Chris remembers so vividly in Part Four. What is Gibbon expressing through such wasteland imagery?

At its simplest, the idea that the day of the crofter is finished. Guthrie thought the world 'rolling fast to hell', and in a way he's right. Gibbon is using the wasteland pattern *in reverse*. In *Sunset Song* no Lawrentian Earth-woman or man, no Corn kings or queens, can propitiate the dark changes taking place. Is he partly mocking or parodying the pattern conventionally used? He surely does not mean us to think that 'Gods' or dark forces are changing the weather, and yet that is what seems to happen. He surely doesn't believe that the sacrifice of a Corn queen (Chris's mother) or king (father) can bring about a good harvest, and yet that is what happens. There is even a ritual fire-ceremony where Chris and Will cleanse the past by burning the whins (in Part Two, 'Drilling'). But although this may 'burn out' the evil memories of Jean Guthrie's death and the remains of Chris's youth, and although the fire at Peesie's Knapp shortly after has a comparable beneficial effect in that (temporarily) Kinraddie makes common cause and all pitch in to help Chae, shortly the rhythms of Kinraddie's decline re-assert themselves. Voices once more set neighbour against neighbour in their scandal-mongering about Mollie Douglas, the minister, and Chae's burning of his own farm. This parody of the usual 'wasteland' pattern is obvious as *A Scots Quair* develops, with its increasing aridity in the city. In Part Four, 'Harvest', a picture of temporary fertility and rural harmony is set in a black historical surrounding. Its good weather and crops are counterpointed by the ironic ideas of bitter harvest on a much vaster scale, that black harvest in the deaths of Ewan, Chae, Rob and Will. This black harvest has despoiled Kinraddie through the ages:

> And the land changes, their parks and steadings are a desolation where the sheep are pastured, we are told that great machines come soon to till the land, and the great herds come to feed on it, the crofter has gone.

Isn't the dark vision only too clear? *Sunset Song* read like this, as picture of a Land being wasted, has little to offer other than Robert's hopeful words. *This* wasteland bodies forth a myth of loss, in which the Corn queen murders her children, the Corn king goes mad amidst his plentiful harvest, and their daughter leaves her beloved land by free choice to follow, in the flesh if not in the spirit, one who represents to her a cloud, a misty irrelevance of modern religion.

Gibbon introduces two running motifs, centred on Chris, to develop this dark vision. The first is a constant preoccupation with death, and almost an obsession with horrific atrocity (which I have elsewhere referred to as 'the Horror' in his work generally); the second a use of the notion of 'dream' (by far and away the most used word in *A Scots Quair*). Consider how often the novel — often unobtrusively, but persistently — reminds us not just of death, but of time which leaves death in its wake, time which is change and thus decay for mere local mortals. This elegy for the dead is the opening note, with its memory of so many long-dead protagonists, leaving only their weathered carvings on stone, which itself crumbles in time.

Events in history are rarely presented as benign or happy. Wars are frequent, with the implication of death on a huge scale, heightened in effect by the distance of time, like Aberlemno Stone with its 'horses and the charging and the rout of those coarse foreign folk', or the account of Flodden 'just as it was told in 'The Floo'rs o' the Forest' which made Chris cry at school 'for the sadness of it and the lads that came back never again to their lasses . . . but . . . lay happed in blood and earth'. Or, growing stronger still, the vivid evocation of the Covenanting folk who 'had screamed and died while the gentry dined and danced' in Dunnottar castle. Again, as so often, the effect is conveyed through crumbling stone, as if to say — if these stones crumble, then how much more mortal is mere flesh! Here, inscribed on a stone which anticipates the memorial stones to the four at the end, with a similar debt to the Book of Revelation, are the names of those Covenanters that Death and Time have claimed. We are to remember them at the end, and see Rob, Ewan, Chae and James Leslie as dying into the common lot of history.

Death in time present is frequent in the novel, reminding us that in the midst of life we are in death. Thus the Guthrie twins are short-lived, and their mother's beauty cut off. When Chris's father is buried his is just another death in many, another standing stone to death:

> . . . folk said that every time the grave-digger stuck his bit spade in the ground some bone or other from the olden time would come spattering out . . . an old enough bit as well, right opposite rose the stone with the cross-bones, maybe all the dead bodies had long mouldered away into red clay.

The mordant humour increases the potency of the dominating idea of mortality. A similar juxtaposition of contrasting idiom makes Chris's wedding — supposed to be the highpoint of her womanly development — a haunting, elegiac occasion. Earlier songs of the physical beauty of women, appropriate to the occasion, give way inexorably to songs ruled by images of poison, winter, the weary world and the death of Auld Robin Gray, ghosts, and with the keening lament of 'The Floo'rs o' the Forest' and 'Auld Lang

Syne' reminding of final departures, anticipating the loss of Will, and the other flowers of manhood of Kinraddie in the Great War.

But death as *idea*, in Chris's mind and conversation, is more insidious and even more important in terms of the trilogy's development. I mean by this the way in which Chris's mind, even from childhood, seems fatally attracted to the point of morbidity, to the state of *non-existence*, to speculation throughout *A Scots Quair* about *not-being*. Again, we meet this first with 'The Floo'rs o' the Forest', which song causes her to write her first significant essay out of her pain and concern with the ancient dead. This is to be repeated, for her next essay praised by teachers (at school in Duncairn) is on 'Deaths of the Great'. While Marget Strachan will joke about 'bodies of men . . . salted and white in great stone vats', Chris takes this to heart and, appalled, sees that the vein beating in her friend's throat:

> would never do that when one was dead and still under grass, down in the earth that smelled so fine and you'd never smell; or cased in the icy darkness of a vat, seeing never again the lowe of burning whins . . . only a fool loved being alive!

She is glimpsing even now the final position she will adopt. On the night before her marriage she sees her mother's dead face and the standing stones, fused in images of terror. Guthrie's funeral and her wedding call forth remarkably similar responses. Her agony of empathy for her dead father reveals an intensity on Gibbon's and her part which is striking, to say the least. And in all these frequent episodes — the visits to Dunnottar and Edzell castles, the vision of Ewan's shattered body at the standing stones, the memorial service at the end, a vitally important point lies concealed: it is Gibbon who is revealing his own obsession with death.

This can be demonstrated by considering just tiny details, representative of the entire *A Scots Quair*. When Will rouses Chris to burn the whins, she says she can't as she has jelly to make. 'Oh, to hell with your jelly, we'll soon be jelly and bones in a grave ourselves, come on!' he cries. Chris's wedding, quite apart from Chris's own thoughts on death, is surrounded, permeated by Gibbon with grotesquely out-of-place images: two rats 'kissing', the wife of the grave-digger, who babbles of 'my first man, him that's

93

now dead', a black ribbon round Chris's neck, and even Mistress Mutch's sleepy advice:

> Take things easy in married life, Chris...Though God knows it'll make not a difference in a hundred years' time and we're dead.

Similarly revealing are figures like John Muir, the gravedigger of Segget, who only has to appear for his motif, his running joke about death, to appear also.

If Chris and Gibbon are haunted by death in *A Scots Quair*, they are equally haunted by what I've called 'the Horror'. It's a related idea, presenting frequent (and sometimes unnecessary) scenes of nightmare, like the death of Old Nell ('her belly ripped like a rotten swede with the stroke of a great curved horn'), and with her mercy killing(!) by Guthrie ('Nell groaned, groaning blood and sweating, and turned away her neck, and father thrust the scythe at her neck, sawing till she died'); or the descriptions of Chris's mother's agony in labour, and Chris's horror at 'towels clairted with stuff she didn't dare look at'; or old Bob's queerly doubled-up body that Chris falls over in the thunderstorm; or her father's sexual advances; or the horrors of Edzell and Dunnottar and France and Rob in the cells. Yes, there is a vital place for shock and vivid, torpor-disturbing detail in the novel, but can one really justify Gibbon's amount of detail? Consider that the Old Nell story is dragged in, since it interrupts pointlessly the anecdote of Will's beating by Guthrie for crying 'Jehovah'. Do we need to know of Nell's agony in such detail? Two paragraphs of horror interrupt — and it seems that they do so only to allow the periodically necessary letting of blood from Gibbon's agonised vision. Similarly, do we accept as probable that god-fearing Guthrie would threaten his son with castration for swearing? And doesn't Gibbon over-dwell on the idea?

> And mind, my mannie, if I ever hear you again take you maker's name in vain, if I ever hear you use that word again I'll libb you. Mind that. Libb you like a lamb.

In recognising the emphasis on death and horror we move close

94

to the reality of the vision of *Sunset Song*. The use of another motif in connection with those I've described takes us to that final vision, the use of the idea of dream.

Here Chris is central. The trilogy is rhythmically punctuated by Chris's 'epiphanies', what appear to be moments of revelation. What is less immediately obvious is the qualification to this — that Chris may instead be creating dreams and new images of herself, illusions which are rhythmically and predictably punctured, and die.

An overused critical comment on the novel has emphasised 'the two Chrisses' of the Land and of books. To remain with this view of her throughout the novel is to ignore the fact that she not only solves this dilemma with the death of her father, but discovers other Chrisses and many more dilemmas throughout *A Scots Quair*. More true to Gibbon's intention is the realisation that Chris travels through many selves and dreams. My question here is — does she *ever* arrive at a final point? The burden of critical opinion suggests that she does, that Chris identifies with the Land and that in dying she completes a movement towards unity with it. My reservation is that while Chris may think this, and indeed a part of Gibbon asserts this, there are deeper creative parts of Gibbon which remain detached and ironic about her positional changes, and about what seems to be her final position.

Chris's 'strange dream' of Pytheas may be 'Great Memory', a perception of her racial origins — or it may be part of her obsession with dream or the dead. Very early on, and shocking in one so young, she thinks 'only a fool loved being alive'. Shortly after, 'nothing endures... Not a thing, though you're over young to go thinking of that'. This is supposed to be Chris thinking, but isn't it Gibbon intruding, preparing us for the later Chris who will have real doubts? With her mother's death Chris makes her first transition from the dream of childhood:

> It was not mother only that died with the twins, something died in your heart and went down with her to lie in Kinraddie kirkyard — the child in your heart died then, the bairn that believed the hills were made for its play... the Chris of the books and the dreams died with it... you folded them up... and laid them away by the dark, quiet corpse that was your childhood.

Actually, neither the Chris of the books or dreams is dead. The first will revive briefly on Guthrie's death, the second has a long road to travel, through many a dream. Only pages later she has begun another dream of how she and her future lover will love one another: 'And maybe that third and last Chris would find voice at last for the whimsies that filled her eyes...'. The 'maybe' and 'whimsies' betray that deep down she already suspects that he may not be the complete answer. 'You may dream of a lad,' she muses — and the next section begins 'So that was the harvest madness that came on Chris...'. But the dream won't go. It's briefly interrupted by the recurrence of the 'old-time dream' at Guthrie's death of going up to college again, but after her father's burial these 'fine bit plannings' disappear, 'just the dreamings of a child over toys it lacked'. Then she falls in love with Ewan. Again she deludes herself that this state will be reality and truth: 'she'd never dream things again, she's live them, the days of dreaming were by... and there was Ewan waiting for her...'.

This happiness (like that of Anna and Will in *The Rainbow*) is seen to be unsustainable. They farm together, they 'play' at being a couple, with Ewan shooting on the moor and returning with rabbits to his woman, but the dream of complete fulfilment has to end, breaking in stages. Ewan eventually has to go back to the outside world:

> But, and it crept into her mind that night and came often in the morning and days that followed, somehow that going of Ewan's to the Mill had ended the foolishness that shut them in fast from Kinraddie and all the world, they two alone, with all the gladness... Kinraddie came in again.

Chris feels at each of these emotional changes, or watersheds, that she has come out of dream permanently — yet subsequent events continually show that many stages lie ahead of her. This is proved by the description of her realisation that she is pregnant, when again she feels that 'dreams were fulfilled and their days put by'.

She is now, temporarily a 'sleeper from dreams', presumably in the sense that she considers herself no longer deluded. But as 'Harvest' begins we see that the alienation which pregnancy had induced between her and Ewan has been yet another nightmare dream. The gap mended between them, she feels 'as though a bank had gone down behind which she had dreamt a torrent and a storm would burst and blind and whelm her. But there was nothing there but the corn growing and the peewits calling. Another 'dream' evaporates behind her, another dead self is laid to rest, and, lest we fail even now to see how changeable she is, by the next page, reconciled with Ewan, she is saying 'dreamily, *maybe things are changing for the better all round*'. Ewan and Chris are now locked fast in a private world, ignoring the war. There's no doubt we're meant to see their peace, their playing with Ewan, and their 'safety' as illusory. Chris watches Ewan and Rob work together. Rob cries 'The Spring of life, eh, Chris...Sing it and cherish it, 'twill never come again!'

> And she heard Ewan call *Ay, man, Rob*, and Rob call *Ay, Man, Ewan*, and they called the truth, they seemed fine men both against the horizon of Spring, their feet laired deep in the wet clay ground, brown and great, with their feet on the earth and the sky that waited behind.

This is the familiar perception of the abiding land (admittedly with the inconsistency on Gibbon's part of raising the agricultural work he elsewhere condemns to epic importance). But Chris:

> looked at them over-long, they glimmered to her eyes as though they had ceased to be there, mirages of men dreamt by a land grow desolate against its changing sky.

Chris of the Land is 'corrected' by another Chris who has intuitive glimpses of timeless truths, who sees eventually that *change* is all and will ultimately master the land. Both of these 'Chrisses' are immediately mastered by the Chris of the family dream:

> And the Chris that had ruled those two other selves of herself, content, unquestioning these many months now, shook her head and called herself daft.

At the very least this demonstrates the flexibility or fragmentation of Chris's self. At most, as I'll argue holds good throughout *A*

Scots Quair, it shows what Chris will end up unable to escape from — the knowledge that all is changed by time, even the land. It is an anticipation of the final dark vision of Gibbon's, and an illustration of Gibbon's own swift changes of mood and belief. For the moment we learn not to accept Chris on the subject of herself, so that when she anticipates Ewan home on leave, happy, inspired by Rob's song (his singing is so important one sometimes is tempted to believe that *his* is the sunset song):

> she dreamt as she listened to that singing, that they'd all be back in Kinraddie as once they'd been, Chae and Long Rob and her dark lad, Ewan himself. So she'd dreamt that morning, she'd never grow out from long dreaming in Autumn dawns like those.

Never? Once again, events shatter the dream. 'Fruition of dream came soon enough,' says Gibbon (or thinks Chris) dryly — in the horror of Ewan, symbolically shorn, the cat-like animal scarred and putrescent, his homecoming 'a nightmare', Chris hurt to the core, 'in a dream'. It gets worse, too, till, after his death, she 'realises' that 'she was living a dream in a world gone mad', and vows to live 'behind the walls of a sanity cold and high, locked in from the lie of life'. This nightmare is of course illusion too. It is fascinating to compare her all-too-brief love with Rob with these 'realisations' — for no great epiphanies are involved, 'she never knew when and how' it came about that she found herself his, 'out of the earth itself, maybe'. The word 'dream' is not used here, where it might so naturally have been employed for such a sudden and unusual occurrence. The significance of this is that with Rob she *has* touched reality and truth, without, perhaps, ever after fully realising it. Certainly one can't argue that by the end of *Sunset Song* she has 'arrived' anywhere. She gives up the Land, her deepest self as she has argued hitherto, to marry the minister of a faith she doesn't share and to sing in his choir! She obviously has much to find out about herself yet, and to this extent *Sunset Song* cannot be regarded as a totally self-contained novel. But before looking at the two following parts, I'd like to argue that already we can see the likely end of her journey, and we can guess at Gibbon's own developing, and we have to accept, altering, vision.

I think this end has been implied in the intensity of the motifs I have already examined. The emphasis on death, the horror in life, the tendency of even so sensitive a person as Chris to dream — all point beyond celebration of the abiding land to a darker conclusion. I agree that Gibbon does convey the sense of an abiding earth, with his descriptions such as Peesie's Knapp having 'the sweat of two thousand years in it', and I have already allowed that he sees the workers of the land as epic, here and in places like his essay, 'The Land'. Like Rob Galt in 'Clay', Long Rob tries nobly to conquer the 'coarse moorland' behind the mill; a daft ploy to the 'speak' of Kinraddie, but not to us, as it underlines the fact that he is of 'the Elder People', the last of the peasants, trying like Rob to 'connect' with his ancestors' way of life. He and Chae and Ewan and Guthrie are 'the wonder of humankind', 'the men who conquered the land and wrung sustenance from it by stealth . . . and endurance'. But then Gibbon goes further and tempers this view by suggesting that though they temporarily control the land, it is the untended land that triumphs, as it did at the end of 'Clay', with the whins and broom reclaiming their stolen territory, creeping down over the land Rob Galt 'unquieted' for so brief a time. This view is put most strongly in Chris's view of the land after her father's death:

> Then a queer thought came to her there in the drooked fields, that nothing endured at all, nothing but the land she passed across, tossed and turned and perpetually changed below the hands of the crofter folk since the oldest of them had set the Standing Stones by the loch of Blawearie . . . Sea and sky and the folk . . . they lasted but as a breath, a mist of fog in the hills, but the land was forever, it moved and changed below you, but was forever.

Apart from the question that rises to mind as to why the sea or the sky should be any less longer lasting than the land, the point is clear. Chris finds her identity with the land. Even more important is that nothing endures. This was first stated in 'Ploughing', but dismissed as being not a fit thought for one so young; repeated as the Greek παντα ρεν 'everything flows on', from Heraclitus's *On Nature*, which argued that the universe is in a state of continuous flux, destining everything (land included) to change. Admittedly Chris qualifies her Greek lesson by adding 'but the land' — but isn't the implication that she can't have her Heraclitus and change him? Ironically, when she does envisage that her marriage is nothing in the immensity of time to follow, and that 'the face of the land (will) change and change again in the coming of the seasons and the centuries till the last lights sank away from it', it is that very element she had said the land would outlast that destroys it, for the continuation of the quotation is 'and the sea came flooding up the Howe, all her love and tears for Ewan not even a ripple of that flood of water far in the times to be'.

We are left in the end with the Stones as memorials to a darkening world, with only the temporary lamp of mens' hearts to ward off — for a while — the night. The novel has been haunted by the cry of lapwings, the birds who have lost their nests at harvest, and cry to find them again, just as Chris will lose hers, and cry, wanting her place on the land again. It has been haunted by stones of castle and graveyard and elder people, standing stones which are indeed Time itself, 'Gnomons of a giant dial . . . creeping into the East' — telling of time running out for life itself. Looked at in this light, the sunset song is elegy for Gibbon's own love for the Land. After all, Gibbon buried himself, or a part of himself (James Leslie) with Rob and Ewan and Chae; James Leslie is both the fourth name on the standing stones and Gibbon's own real name, James Leslie Mitchell. Now he moves forward to consider the humanist idealist, Robert Colquohoun, representative of another way of looking at life's riddle. Already cloud imagery is creeping in over the sun, as the ending to 'Harvest': 'the snipe stilled their calling, a cloud came over the sun'. Chris has seen shadows over the sun and metaphorically in her life light. The 'Epilude' brings 'the clouds sailing down from the North and over the sun'; Robert is given the last statement, uttering his belief in what Chris will see as the great Cloud he follows, hoping 'that the new oppressions and foolish greeds are no more than mists that pass'.

Chris will be oddly passive from now on, her major act in *Cloud Howe* fruitless in every sense, since it robs her of her child. I believe that Gibbon has let her be the vital centre of *Sunset Song*, but has shown and will show that her way is not enough. What of Robert's? *A Scots Quair* is a trilogy which mirrors decline, Gibbon's 'Decline and Fall' of healthy community man. *Sunset Song* works because it lives off the richness remaining in Kinraddie community, but it has, as I've shown, a dark side showing the movement to a life-style of greedy egotism and exploitation of land and people. I want to suggest now that *Cloud Howe* and *Grey Granite* enact successfully *all that Gibbon wishes them to enact*. They are rich in symbolism and meaning if we allow that Gibbon moves on to show, in Robert and then in Ewan, two ways *beyond* Chris, beyond the Sunset of healthy community. Seen this way, *A Scots Quair* grows in stature even from that large conception of its being Chris Caledonia's, Scotland's, story from tribalism and peasantry to the rule of church and Reformation to Industrial Revolution, as well as physical movement from village to town to city. It now becomes the movement of mankind, an outline of history portrayed through Scottish characters and archetypes, with the three basic human metaphysical responses to life. First there is Land-based stoic and passive endurance, abolishing illusion and dream and accepting a meaningless Cosmos. Then Gibbon assesses various creeds and 'Cloud'-based religion, be they Christianity or whatever. Finally — and it's crucial to see that Gibbon does *not* mean us to see this as yet another 'dream' or 'cloud' — he postulates the only conceivable third way, that which Chris wonders about in the middle of *Cloud Howe*. Her conjectures are central to the entire trilogy:

> The men of the earth that had been, that she'd known, who kept to the earth and their eyes upon it . . .

(This is Chris herself and her Elder People, after-voice of the 'Golden Age'.)

> the hunters of clouds that were such as was Robert; how much was each wrong and how much each right?

Chris then concludes with the question:

> and was there maybe a third way to Life, unguessed, unhailed, never dreamed of yet?

Yes, there is; and it isn't unguessed or unhailed, since Gibbon

101

shows elsewhere that it almost worked with Spartacus and Wallace, figures who did not identify with creeds but with their fellow-men, who were their fellow-men in their suffering. They were leaders and realists who accepted that they might fail and, unlike Robert, were not broken by the realisation of the possibility or the event.

Robert is the centre of *A Scots Quair*, since an undeniable fact usually overlooked is that he, not Chris, sums up the end of Kinraddie and he ushers in Ewan and the replacement for Christianity and clouds, the 'stark sure creed that will cut like a knife through the doubt and disease' which 'men with unclouded eyes' may yet find. But he will not deny Christ either; he will have a vision of him at his death, and *Chris* will speak with Christ's voice, 'It is finished' — that is, the dream is finished that the creed of Christianity can on its own establish Goodness and Love on the earth. The position of Christ at the end of *Cloud Howe* is that of 'Forsaken'; his dream may be spent, but he is recognised and not despised by the communist family.

Thus I defend the later *Quair* novels on the score that their meaning and symbolic presentation is clear and artistically very rich. They lack the metaphor of country and vivid 'speak', but that is partly because the world which gave the richness is dead. Part of their theme of impoverishment is bodied forth in the thin texture of natural description, the nastiness of their social intercourse, and the way in which their structure and pattern becomes a parody of that of *Sunset Song*. But they *are* lesser novels. They over-concentrate on the three figures of Robert, Chris and Ewan. Chris mechanically creaks into her *Sunset Song*/standing stones position of recollection at the beginning of each section of each of the two last novels. This habit 'fixes' Chris too predictably, along with increasing amounts of cliche writing (Ewan's 'blue helmet' of hair, his coolness endlessly asserted, the flint and Golden Age connection done to death; Chris's 'nice' legs', 'nice hair', 'sulky mouth'; John Muir's grave-littered remarks; Dite Peat's unvarying dirty sadism: Ake's angry wasted sneering poetry). All this reveals that Gibbon is tired and straining to give the world a message. It is the triumph of propaganda over art which spoils these last novels, although I would argue that at least the propagandist vision gives a unity of rich symbolism as consolation for loss. The trouble is that symbolic figures like Robert or Ewan must also fit their context of a naturalistic novel portraying what are supposed to be real places and people. Thus Robert becomes implausible and Ewan's superhuman restraint and coolness and leadership unbelievable. Gibbon managed in *Spartacus* — but significantly he distanced his leader in time, adopted a style close to that of fable, and managed thus to surround the epic symbolic figure with an atmosphere of legend, so that he fitted. Robert and Ewan don't fit.

The final flaw in these two novels is in that dark under-vision which Gibbon just kept in check and balance in *Sunset Song*, that 'Horror' which I've argued is the final position of a writer obsessed with Death.

In *Cloud Howe* it is significant that Robert's 'emblems' are clouds, dreams, the manse yew trees (traditionally associated with malevolent witchcraft, spared when the protective conifers of Kinraddie and the Mearns are stripped for war), and his old bike, on its last legs by the end of the novel. All in their way suggest his worth and its limitations. The Clouds Robert follows are those of Exodus 13; 20–22:

> And they (Moses and the Children of Israel) took their journey...and encamped...in the edge of the Wilderness. And the Lord went before them by day in a pillar of a cloud, to lead them the way.

This is the text of Robert's Armistice day sermon. Robert's Christianity is very much of a self-help kind:

> And he said that God had made neither night nor day in human history. He'd left it in the hands of Man to make both, God was but Helper, was but Man himself... God also had died in the holocaust in the fields of France. But he rose anew, Man rose anew, he was as undying as God was undying — if he had the will and the way to live... *A pillar of cloud by day and a pillar of fire by night* — they had hung in the sky since the coming of men, set there by God.

Putting the two quotations together yields much of Robert's faith. Man can be led from the corrupt civilisation (Pharaoh's

103

Egypt, Western man's modern imperialism leading to the 1914–18 'holocaust') through the wilderness (it will be a long uphill struggle, as Ewan will say also) to the Promised Land. (One remembers that Moses was given only the view of the Land from Mount Pisgah, just as Robert and Ewan see only glimpses.) Chris has already questioned this — but it is a question allowing an open answer — 'his dream just a dream? Was there a new time coming to the earth, when nowhere a bairn would cry in the night, or a woman go bowed as her mother had done, or a man turn into a tormented beast?' Robert's Christianity is linked with his practical programme the same way that *Spartacus* links Warrior-Leader and Christ together in Kleon's vision at the end. As he enthuses to Chris, the Kingdom of God and St Augustine's City of Gold are to be built in this world, not the next. This is important, since it shows that Robert rejects much of the motivating principles of the Reformation and Calvinism, in so far as that crucial to them was the notion that this world was a Vale of Tears, and that all happiness lay beyond the trial and temporary earthly state. He's close indeed to many a modern Ecumenicist in his emphasis that 'Christ was no Godlet, but a leader and a hero'. Again, as he enthuses thus to Chris at the Standing Stones atop Culdyce moor in 'Stratus', he enunciates the principles of Diffusionism. All three Gibbon dogmas now co-exist quite happily. Robert is Diffusionist, Christian and socialist, a secular-religious trinity, all at once here, as he dreams of how the May strike of 1926 will free men and return the Golden Age *and* bring God's City to earth.

It doesn't. The league of the Segget spinners collapses with the General Strike and Robert breaks. His sickness makes him revert to the 'Blood of the Lamb' form of Christianity where he argues salvation within rather than without, traditional Reformed Christianity, until the Ratworld manifests itself in its most horrid form so far by devouring the child of Kindness. The symbolism is right on the edge of melodrama, and yet, so simply presented is it that the parallel of the Kindness family finding no room at any inn or house at Christmas with the birth of Christ is acceptable and moving. This travesty of the Christ-child's story reverses Robert's retreat into 'safe' religion, and he finishes *Cloud Howe*, as he did *Sunset Song*, with a sermon which is not just meant to show his limitations. He *is* a powerful voice speaking for Gibbon, and I would draw attention to the fact that he has not so much lost his Christianity as declared it temporarily useless. Far from losing it, he actually sees Christ for the first time, and Christ speaks. This may seem both impossible and unlikely, but I draw the reader's attention to his sermon. A cloudless, icy weather presages it; the wasteland is very much with us. His text is from St Luke, concerning the penitent thief who asked Christ to remember him when he came into his Kingdom. It is double-edged in its irony. (The other thief had asked Christ to save them, if he was really Christ. The penitent thief said no; they, the two thieves, were justly in their predicament.) Thus Robert says to Christ that he has no obligation to save humanity from its neglect of the Kindnesses (and of Faith, Hope, and Charity, these neglected virtues of Kinraddie church). But he also goes further, arguing that 'there is no hope for the world at all — as I, the least of his followers see — except it forget the dream of the Christ... and turn and seek with unclouded eyes... a stark, sure creed that will cut like a knife.'

It's important to see that he is still a follower; that he sees the stark creed as bringing about the possibility of 'the Christ come back', 'far off yet in the times to be'. A moratorium has been declared on the practice of the faith, not a total repudiation.

Now, like Kleon dying at the end of Spartacus Robert has his genuine vision:

> Robert had stopped, the queer look on his face. For he stared down the kirk as though Someone stood there. And then a bright crimson thing came on his lips.

There is no doubt in my mind that this is meant to be a valid vision. It is Gibbon who puts the capital at 'Someone', and Gibbon who implies a pulling back of the curtain. It's stranger yet — for Chris of all people, cloudless Golden Age Woman, speaks for the Christ himself, who in St John 19:30 'gave up the ghost' with the words she uses, 'It is finished'.

Chris 'heard herself speak, in strange words not her own, unbidden to her lips'. And Chris's last gesture in Segget is, 'queerly', a Christian blessing upon it. The sunset of Christianity has fallen. We remember that Robert's *Sunset Song* sermon gave 'the Morning Star', the possibilities of Christ, to Kinraddie and the post-war world. *Cloud Howe* uses the image of the falling star frequently, atmospherically and metaphorically showing Christianity and Robert in decline, unable to meet the needs of a desperate world. Robert had thought that Freedom and God would come together. Now he sees, on his death, that Freedom must come first. Ewan must take up his creed, strengthened both by being the living descendant of the Golden Age Robert admired so much and by having the clear vision of the New Man.

Cleverly Gibbon has kept the notion of creeds, warring sets of beliefs, as the unifying notion of the novel. Airy notions and pointless changes of direction are seen not just in Robert but in many others, like Mowat and his Scottish Nationalism, blowing hot for a spell, then chilling into the Fascism of Italy of 1930; or the Cronins and their socialism, as soon blown out in Jock Cronin and his movement up the social scale. Gibbon satirises Ramsay MacDonald, compromiser *par excellence*, and Social Credit, Major Douglas's scheme for all to have shares in the wealth of the country by birthright, popular with Scottish Nationalists like MacDiarmid and Mackenzie. Toryism is so frequently mocked that it's the warp and woof of Gibbon's satiric portrayal of New Toun Segget, from the foolish jingoism of the Misses McAskill and Ferguson, to Mrs Geddes's belief in basket-work and socials in the W.R.I. (Women's Rural Institute). It is the role of Chris and Ewan, as yet undivided in attitudes, to suggest the hollowness of these creeds and Gibbon's darkest vision.

Through Chris, beyond all consideration of Christianity, Diffusionism and communism, we perceive the deepest layer of Gibbon's striated vision. We continue with Chris to shed illusions and dreams. To this extent the Cloud section titles reflect her progress as much as Robert's, so that temporarily in 'Cirrus' she has set aside her dead and her memories — 'she'd not think of that, part of the old, sad dream that was done'. She enters her new 'dream' with Robert, but significantly she never again gives herself totally. Always one has the awareness of Chris's self as an enclosed, self-protecting ring — perhaps symbolised in the ring of standing stones or embattlements of Kaimes Castle which are her refuge, just as her final refuge, unable to find such in the Windmill Braes of Duncairn, is in the 'high, cleared space' of the ancient astronomers on the hill-top above Cairndhu. She looks at her sleeping Robert, 'brows set dark in a dream', and perceives the distance and the danger between them. This isn't the naive young Chris, but one who 'plays', temporarily but without deep convictions, with dream. The question remaining is — how far is her beloved Land still valid compensation?

To an extent it still sustains her. For example on removal to Segget the talk with the 'fee'd man' who remembers Echt and her father delights her, and she's once again filled with the pattern of her old life, remembering:

> the rocks were cawing up in the yews, and you thought how they'd fringed your pattern of life-birds, and the waving leafage of trees; peewits over the lands of Echt... spruce... that climbed up the slopes to the Barmekin bend; snipe sounding low on Blawearie loch... the whisp of the beech out by the hedge in the quiet of the night.

Gibbon uses that dark word 'dream' twice for this delight, introducing it, and ending it, when 'she shook herself and came out of her dream'. It's just after this, sitting at the Kaimes at the end of 'Cirrus', that she wonders whether Robert is merely dreamer, or whether indeed a new time may come for the earth. That is, she is still capable of wondering whether she's on the right track. She is still capable of being 'lifted' or depressed by Robert, especially by the extremes of his hopefulness or his 'black moods'. One of these in 'Cumulus' precipitates *her* dark vision:

> So, in the strangest of moments it would come, in a flame and a flash... You'd see... the hopeless folly of all striving, all hope.

She 'sees' her father's bones, she realises he's totally forgotten, and she has her first Land-consuming vision of what lies beyond the earth. Robert has argued that we all come from earth:

> but wilder and stranger you knew it by far, from the earth's beginning *you yourself* had been here, a blowing of motes in the world's prime, earth, roots, and the wings of an insect long syne in the days when the dragons still ranged the world

— every atom in your body now ... these had been here,
there was nothing but a change, in a form, the stroke and the
beat of a song.

This is an important passage for the understanding of *Cloud
Howe*. Chris's fundamental honesty has taken her past 'nothing
endures but the land' to a perception that even the earth is subject
to time and atomic change. It is as yet '*a change*', and not *Change*,
and she still tends to equate Earth with Reality. She still doesn't accept that death is the end of all, wanting a shallow grave so that her
atoms may yet dance with the Land.

Nevertheless, in 'Cumulus' we can see that she has taken on
much of the burden of the Death-and-Horror theme, rather than
being the Dreamer, which is now Robert's role. Awareness of
Robert's hideous war-wound brings 'the Horror' flooding into her
mind, and she 'put that dream by, the dream of a bairn fathered by
Robert' — although as so often, she's inconsistent, since she does
have his child, short-lived.

A measure of Chris's progress can be seen by comparing her with
Miss Jeannie Grant, the socialist schoolteacher who is close to what
Chris of the Books-dream, English Chris, would have become if
things had been different — 'young and earnest, and Chris half-
liked her, as though she stood on a hill and looked down on her
own youth only beginning to climb, half-liking its confidence, pi-
tying its blindness'. Chris has one place in the novel, and in *A Scots
Quair* it's the last time, where she speaks with political commitment and anger. This is when she speaks out against Mowat and his
Fascism. It's an odd passage, because it suddenly reminds us just
how long it's been since she did speak out. One wonders why it's
taken her so long, and why she even needs to say 'if it came to the
push' she'd choose the spinners. Isn't it so obvious that she would,
that she's of the folk? The answer to why she has been so quiet so
long lies in her sudden coolness after speaking — 'a daft blether of
words' she thinks. Suddenly yet again we see that she's *limited*, she
lacks either Robert's passionate concern or Ewan's shrewd recognition of man's inhumanity to man. For part of her reason for thinking herself daft is that she thinks that the cruelty won't come again,
that 'there would never come back that old darkness again to torment the simple folk of her blood'. This is Chris evading the rea

108

world that Robert and Ewan engage with. She withdraws into self, coolness, and a *laissez-faire* attitude which is not so much hypocrisy as a knowledge that if she's really pushed, beyond matters of voting, say, she hasn't much time for humanity or even existence anyway. What we are witnessing in *Cloud Howe*, and what this passage shows us, is the transition of Chris from member of the Folk to Chris Alone. It's not that she's too stupid to see that the days of Horror for ordinary people aren't over — it's just that she's moving to a point where she doesn't care, which explains her running expression throughout *Cloud Howe* and *Grey Granite* of weariness and age. She feels old and tired because she sees life as sound and fury, meaning nothing. It is very significant that now, at the end of 'Cumulus' and beginning of 'Stratus', exactly half-way through *A Scots Quair* as well as the novel, she is displaced by Ewan as the main point of view. She will look back, Ewan forward. Now she writes her name on the graveyard wall, looking back over her dead selves, Chris after Chris, and rubbing out her name.

One of the problems of dealing critically with Gibbon's presentation of Chris is that we tend to accept whatever she's saying or thinking at any time rather than seeing that they are the limited and temporary perceptions of a character created like all the other characters in the novel. When she now sees life as 'the flicker of the little folk that came and builded and loved and hated and died, and were not, a crying and swarm of midges warmed by the sun to a glow and a dance', the temptation to accept this as Gibbon and Chris in final verdict is strong. We should resist, since neither Gibbon or Chris is being final. Within four pages of 'Nimbus' we can see this, with Chris wishing that she were as sure as Ewan was of himself, to go her own way, to be 'a million things — Christ — alone, Christ — herself, with Chris Guthrie, Chris Tavendale, Chris Colquohoun dead!' Yet almost immediately after this was read that, climbing the moors with Cis Brown, sitting on a great stone of antique times, she is 'aloof and sure and untroubled by things'. Once again we see the moving Chris, now dreaming her old dream of 'the Real', as she now says, 'unstirred and untouched', but followed by the hesitant qualification, so typically Chris's — 'surely if that were not also a dream' — which the deepest part of Gibbon and Chris suggests it is. This trip to the moor has given her some knowledge of herself — 'lost maybe herself, but she followed no cloud, be it named or unnamed', but she still does not know whether there is anything 'between the Clouds and the Howe'. In a mythical sense Chris is the Earth Mother whose time is past.

Ewan is now the source of energy for the book, the 'New Man' — no longer the simple 'Corn king' necessary to revivify the land, but the 'way undreamt of', a superman who is Chris *and* Robert, the something between the Clouds and the Howe. The problem about Ewan for Gibbon is that Ewan is impossible. He has to fit into a novel about 'real' people like Chae and John Muir and real history like that of the depression of the 1930s. Gibbon is far less successful evoking the feelings of this superboy than he has been with human Chris, which is odd considering that Ewan is presumably close to Gibbon's own boyhood in the love of flints, the cool separateness from family, the instinctive awarenesss of superiority over others. Herein may lie the trouble. Ewan becomes self-indulgent. Gibbon fills him with the qualities he'd like himself to have had, and wants his leader of men to have, without maintaining Ewan's credibility. All the 'Stratus' passages from Ewan's point of view imply an impossible wisdom beyond his years, and an amazing understanding of people.

Gibbon doesn't mean him to come over as priggish and unnaturally cold, but since he is the product of Gibbon's speculative political mind it is inevitable that, as Leader-elect, his relationships with girls and friends must be secondary to his Messianic purpose, the theme of *Grey Granite*.

Grey Granite tries to keep the pattern of the previous novels. The Windmill Braes provide the opening location for each chapter, with Chris mulling over recent events in the way she did before at the standing stones or Kaimes Castle. Political songs replace Segget's rhymes, and at the novel's heart the New Year dance which humanises Ewan is paralleled in the wedding of Chris in *Sunset Song* and the Segget dance. The 'speak' is still here too, as voice of the suffering worker. But none of these is as convincing as before. The Braes give little comfort to Chris, rather reminding her of age and weariness and city impersonality. The songs are travesties of Rob's old music, the 'speak' hysterical rather than evocative (although it and the dance have vitality).

110

Partly at least this is deliberate, to show the decline of communi-ty quality. Even the opening pages show this purpose, with images of wasteland slime, decay and death surrounding Chris on the Braes. Nevertheless, Gibbon seems to fail on three counts. The first is that he over-edits and melodramatises the city experience so that its humour, warmth and value disappear, leaving only the drones, simpletons and snobs of Ma Cleghorn's guesthouse, the Holy Willie minister McShilluck, the utterly corrupt baillies and the brutal policeman. The second is that his style frequently becomes flat and unconvincing, with Chris overdrawn as tired (when at other times she's presented as a desirable, golden-haired 38) and a mood of Gibbon's own desolation colouring her to the point where she becomes wearisomely lack-lustre. The third is connected to this through the stylistic irritations, whereby Ewan is presented as prig-gish, cool, black-haired noble hunter *ad nauseam*. Ewan as convin-cing human being never lives up to Ewan as *Spartacus* — symbol of the Seed-carrier, the New Man, the trapped sunlight at the heart of the crystals of Zircon-Granite.

I do not, however, share the view that the meaning of the novel is unclear, split between the values of Chris and Ewan. Nor do I see Chris as representing Gibbon's final meaning in the book. Increas-ingly I see Gibbon's meaning clearly bodied forth in his symbolic pattern, and in the roles of the Chris and Ewan.

Once again the chapter titles contain much of the meaning. 'Epidote', 'Sphene', 'Apatite' and 'Zircon' are secondary minerals found in Granite. Like MacDiarmid (with whom he was in frequent letter correspondence at this time in connection with *Scottish Scene*), Gibbon had become fascinated by the ideas which geology implied — ideas of vast, impersonal tracts of space-time, where, underneath the changing face of the earth and its bickering human termentors, chemical and crystal change remained the final, endur-ing process. For both men, such thought offered consolation, replacing the hurtful human world of decay with an inhuman time-scale. But Gibbon, unlike MacDiarmid, had to find a link between such thoughts and the human condition. In different ways Chris and Ewan are the links. The meaning of the chapter-titles emerges through them.

Ewan in particular *is* Grey Granite, come also to a city of Grey Granite, which Gibbon in 'Aberdeen' called 'one of the most en-

111

during and indestructible and appalling building materials in use on our planet'. The description fits Ewan also. *Cloud Howe* told us of his love of the flints of the elder people and went further. Ewan was:

> rather like a flint himself . . . but of a better shape and grain, grey granite down to the core . . . with its flinty shine and its cool grey skin and the lights and the flashing strands on it.

Ewan has gone beyond Chris and her link with land. The green living corn of Kinraddie has given way in him to the sedimentary rock beneath. If Chris is the Earth-Goddess, the Land itself, Ewan is something deeper: mineral. And a mineral is formed by the inorganic processes of nature. Chris is organic, but doomed to change and decay. Ewan is still natural, but part of a different and slower time-process.

'Epidote' is an 'impure' and 'metamorphic' element of granite. That is to say, in terms of Ewan's development, he is not yet crystallised into his pure or final shape, and he is liable to change. The mineral is green, and refracts light; it is dense and heavy. Ewan is 'green', linked still with Segget and Kinraddie and his flints, when he comes to Duncairn. He is aloof, refracting into himself the 'light' or influences which will later change him. But he is himself, therefore of 'weight'. 'Sphene' is a mineral which goes to the making of industrial alloys, mainly titanium. Ewan works with just such in Gowan and Gloag's, with materials not found in nature. The name, from Greek, means 'a wedge'. Like Spartacus, who fought always with his 'cuneus wedges' of men, Ewan forms his wedge in the Young League which is to bring together socialist and communist, 'Sphene' is both green and light — as in Ewan, as he perceives his naivety the hard way, through failure and violence. 'Apatite' is greenest, lightest and most transparent of these minerals. Its name means 'the betrayer'; and Ewan is twice betrayed; by Alick Watson at work, and in his faith in Ellen Johns, who is willing to compromise her socialism for her personal satisfaction. Like Spartacus, Ewan learns that the true leader must trust no-one and deny claims of family. Yet he must put his heart in a faith so that although he must die and Change survive, so the movement will progress to Light.

This last is important. As we have seen, Christianity did not die with Robert. Frequently when Ewan feels the changes which crystallise him he reacts in a way we have seen just before this novel in *Spartacus*. Ewan feels 'something that rose and slew coolness and judgement — steady, white-edged, a rising flame . . . as though 'twas yourself that history had tortured . . . and you gave a queer sob that startled yourself: Something was happening to you: God — what? . . .'

This is in 'Sphene'; 'Apatite' shows us Ewan's mind as it 'trembled on the verge of something, something that he couldn't name, maybe God, that made this strange play with lives and beliefs'. Ewan is no cold machine. *He is Spartacus*, undergoing the self-same transformation that Spartacus endured. And both find a kind of God, the 'third way' Chris guessed at, not to be called God by either. This is crucial, otherwise the final exchange about Freedom and God between Chris and Ewan will make no sense. Gibbon postulates a 'higher third way' that Ewan will equate with Freedom, in the sense that pursuit of this way, as Spartacus found with his slave army, is pursuit of the only Freedom worth having. Ewan *becomes* the slave horde, like Spartacus, becomes the 'keelie' he's offended by in the beginning. He thus becomes the 'something' that is the nearest he'll get to God. He becomes 'Zircon', hardest and heaviest of the Granite minerals, its name meaning 'gold-colour', its nature gem-like. He has gone through the full change Chris noticed in 'Apatite' when she saw in him 'change working its measure as sunlight on granite bringing out the gleams of gold and red through the cold grey glister'. He is now trapped, crystallised, sunlight. Thus the song may have had its sunset, but in Ewan the light is the seed which he will carry on, the seed-bearer of the new Golden Age.

Thus Gibbon's message for those after his death. The trouble was that his master-plan for this novel was conceived too logically, too formally, from his head. His heart, or his deepest feelings, remained with Chris, so that finally we see the strange spectacle of Chris who is not actually carrying the positive message of the novel, carrying more emotional conviction, even although theoretically she's of the Past, symbol of the phase of the Land that humanity has outworn. Gibbon means us to see Chris as having no relevance to the movement forward, in the end failing to understand the 'antrin' changes she sees in Ewan. She is seen always in retreat in this

113

novel, harking back to her standing stones, in a way Grey Granite herself, but symbolised by stones which have no inorganic future. They are dead granite as opposed to Ewan's crystallising process of change. This is what Gibbon meant us to see, the dying Earth-Goddess who cannot go where her son goes.

Of course he manages instead to give her an elegiac weight, a nostalgic power, which gives to her end what David Craig describes a terrible desolate thrill, signifying nothing. Craig attacks the novel for this; I disagree with the criticism. In the end Gibbon's familiar, fundamental honesty asserts itself, and the 'horror' and despair about the meaning of life become the dominant closing chords. In 'Apatite' she saw 'SHE HAD NOTHING AT ALL, she never had anything, nothing in the world she'd believed in but change . . . nothing endured.' This horrid vision of a mechanistic universe winding down is echoed shortly after when she broods on the anniversary of Robert's death, and in 'Zircon' when, at the top of the Barmekin she has the vision of 'Change like a hirpling clock, with only benediction to ring at the end — knowledge that the clock would stop some time, that even change might not endure.' She is now devoid of hope or temptation, hate or love. And lest we think that something remains, a Land-link which will sustain her, her death is prefigured by her final vision that everything — Land, dreams, or love — passes:

> her little shelter in Cairndhu a dream of no-life that could not endure. And that was the best deliverance of all . . . that Change who rules the earth and the sky and the waters underneath the earth, Change whose face she'd once feared to see . . . passed and re-passed in the ways of the wind, Deliverer, Destroyer, and Friend in one.

There is no place in the world for an honesty like this. Chris (and Gibbon, one is tempted to add) must (however improbable we think it that a healthy 39-year-old should sit in the cold rain till she dies) pass from it.

Thus the final exchange between Ewan and Chris becomes clear. Gibbon meant the argument to reveal that Chris cannot see what the New Man Ewan can see, that finally both of them are for the freedom of man, passive or active, against the warping creeds dif-

114

fused through time and the world in the name of God. Ewan and Chris are on the side of Freedom, if Chris could only realise what Ewan was doing. But such is the emotive power that Gibbon has vested in Chris, and so genuinely does she reflect that side of his personality given to the Horror and despair, that in the end she dominates. Despair has conquered Hope.

5 *The Silver Darlings* and the Song of Life

Lewis Grassic Gibbon made his *A Scots Quair* the sum of three separate novels. *The Silver Darlings* in its own way is part of a trilogy also, the earlier parts being *Sun Circle* and *Butcher's Broom*. Each of these told of a crucial period in the history of the north-east. The first described the impact of Christianity and Vikings on the age-old Pictish and Druid tribes, the second the social and spiritual changes after the Jacobite Rebellions of the eighteenth century as the clan systems were broken up and the old com-munities of crofters were ejected to make way for more profitable sheepfarming. *The Silver Darlings* takes up the theme of *Butcher's Broom*, which ended in Colin returning from the wars to find his home wasted and his people dispersed. Catrine and Tormad of *The Silver Darlings* are Colin's children — not, of course, literally but in terms of being his people, further on in time and forced to take up a miserable residence next to the North Sea, an element they don't really know. In a way Gunn means the pun 'at sea' to open the novel. The title of the first chapter, 'The Derelict Boat', has a double meaning, in the sense that the poor crofters of inland Caithness and *Butcher's Broom* are derelict too, stranded on the shores of an unfriendly ocean.

Catrine (19) and Tormad (24) are just married. They live in poverty in Dale, near Helmsdale (still a fair fishing port) in Caithness. It is 1816, and Napoleon is in St Helena. Throughout Europe and Britain these are bad years and the press-gang is still ac-tive. It takes Tormad, leaving Catrine pregnant, ignorant of what has happened to him — though she somehow 'knows' he's dead. She leaves Dale for Dunster (Dunbeath) and a new life. There she stays for the next twenty years trying to keep Finn from the sea. Since she does not know formally that Tormad is dead, she is not free to marry Roddie, the youngest skipper of a fishing boat in Dunster. Roddie and Dunster take advantage of the Government's bounty on every cran of herring exported to begin what becomes the saving of the people of the north and east of Scotland — the great nineteenth-century herring fishing, which stretched from Thurso and Wick in the north southwards as far as Anstruther in Fife. Its effects were felt throughout Scotland and beyond. Tiny Dunster, by 1835, had 73 boats out. The fishing was a regeneration, a 'fabulous time'. In this magical atmosphere young Finn grows up drawn inexorably towards the forbidden sea. His friends and their fathers would be going to sea in thirteen open boats, without cover from rain and storm, far into the North Sea. Finn is torn between loyalty towards his mother who wants him to croft, and his own need to discover himself. Catrine and Roddie are also torn: Catrine realising that she is smothering her boy, and drawn reluctantly towards Roddie; Roddie, because he respects Catrine's sorrow for Tormad and her need to wait for the news of his fate. All three have lonely journeys, and the novel is about all of them and their delicate, strong and complex relationships. Finn and Roddie go to sea after Catrine has lifted her prohibition. For a while Finn is content to share the comradeship of the crew of the *Seafoam*, with epic adventures. But as Finn moves from boyhood he increasingly feels Roddie as rival — to himself in adventures, and to himself in his relationship with his mother. The novel is about how Finn comes to terms with this jealousy.

The novel is in parts, each part having a different emphasis, a different music. Music is an important element in Gunn's development of theme and the term 'symphonic' is entirely appropriate to *The Silver Darlings*. Gunn has an overall theme or movement to which the lesser parts of movements are related and subservient. Within these parts motifs, images like rowan berries or birch trees or circles of ancient stones, remind us constantly of the larger, overall theme, arising as they do surprisingly and repeatedly, leading always towards the great unifying closing chords.

Gunn did not formally separate his epic into its three parts. There are chapter headings, which are always significant and helpful, but the great trio of movements which give the book its symphonic shape are not labelled. To have done so would have detracted from the sense of time and life moving forward like the waves of the sea itself, organic and inseparable. Part One runs from Chapter One, 'The Derelict Boat' to Chapter Thirteen, 'Ordeal by

Plague'. Part Two starts Chapter Fourteen, 'Out to Sea', and finishes in Chapter Twenty-nine, 'Sea Love'. Part Three starts with 'Finn goes to Helmsdale' and ends with Chapter Twenty-six, 'Finn in the Heart of the Circle'.

The progress of Gunn's novels is from disruption and disharmony to unity and harmony. In this novel that progress has three stages. Part One shows a land-based people out of their depth at sea, and throughout that part the sea is looked at from the land, expressed through Catrine. Part One is land *and* woman, since broadly we see events from Catrine's point of view. This part ends when Catrine realises that death can also happen on land, since the cholera plague takes another of her dearest, Kirstie. Her balance is restored, and Finn is released to Part Two, to sail with the *Seafoam*. Part Two is dominated by the sea; we look now at the land from it; and this part is also man dominated. But it is, like the land in the first section, only a part of life, and if Catrine was obsessive about the land, then Finn is now obsessive about the sea. Where Catrine shut out the world of men, Finn shuts out memories of his mother and Una. The motif used to illustrate this part is that of the ship in its 'wooden dream', and all the metaphors and adventures suggest a time of enchantment and heroic saga, moving from 'Thorstown' (Thurso) to the Cliff of the Seven Hunters. Part Three sees Roddie settled with Catrine, thus moving sea and land, man and woman, together, Finn still resists his fate, although his deepest self is in fact moving him steadily towards 'the heart of the circle'. Parts One and Two, then, are balanced opposites; with Part Three as resolution of their opposition, harmonious and triumphant.

This terse list of parts reveals nothing of the texture of Gunn's art. It is worth looking at the first chapter more closely than the others, to see how Gunn makes every detail fit both the local theme of despair and tragedy and the overall theme of regeneration.

Tormad and Catrine are sympathetically evoked as young lovers, with comedy lying just above the deeper ominous notes of the prevailing images of death and disruption. Their closeness speaks directly to the reader; what calls for comment is the way that everything that happens has *symbolic* meaning. The chapter title should warn us against taking the apparently cheerful opening at face value — and is it mere coincidence that Gunn makes Tormad spill the pot of limpets into the fire? The idea of discord is developed as we realise that this is no ordinary parting, that under this bantering surface deep feelings are moving. Already the key words 'barren' and 'arid', referring to the land and to Catrine's spirit, begin to dominate, with frequent references to death, and to the gauntness of land and people. Already, too, two ways of regarding the peoples' tragedy are suggested: that they are being punished with poverty (and Napoleon, the 'anti-Christ') for their sins, or that they are the innocent victims of a corrupt outside world, whose lives 'had been pleasant and inoffensive in their loved inland valleys' before the Clearances. Already, too, Gunn shows his deep difference from Gibbon's strident social anger in his quiet willingness to see that this history is not to be read simplistically, with blame and praise given in black and white to landlord and peasant respectively. 'Yet it was out of that very sea that hope was now coming to them. The landlord who had burned them out in order to have a suitable desolation for sheep, had set about making a harbour at the mouth of the river' — admittedly with his own interest in mind; but Gunn recognises the paradox, just as the paradox of happiness emerging from tragedy will come to dominate the book.

The theme of this first chapter is that the hour may have come, but the man has not. This is not to belittle Tormad, whose courage lives on through the book, but he is not Roddie. Indeed he is in contrast to Roddie's Sutherland and Viking fairness with his Pictish darkness and heavy breadth. 'Tormad's heels sank into the earth'; Tormad's element was the strath and land. 'A small wave splashed over his feet and he pulled them out smartly as if he had been stung, just saving himself from falling'. The sea here is seen as alien, hostile; the amount of money being made 'seemed to them uncanny . . . as if some evil chance must be lurking somewhere, ready to pounce'.

Gunn very unobtrusively makes his fishermen describe the sea in land terms, thus betraying their unsureness. They touch their boat 'as if it were a strange horse'. Tormad has 'bull-shoulders', and when they look back to shore (after an awkward start) 'the folk were like small animals, like little dark calves'. Gunn also captures the sense of sea agoraphobia by the same method:

They changed places in the boat so warily that she scarcely

rocked. . . . Not until that moment did they fully realise that they were by themselves, cut off, on the breast of the ocean. They had never before been so far from land, and the slow movement of the sea became a living motion under them. It brimmed up against the boat and choked its own mouth, then moved away, without end, slow, heedless, and terrible, its power restrained, like the power in some great invisible bull. Fear, feather light, kept them wary, like the expectancy of a blow in a dark place.

Not only do the rhythms of the sentences capture the sea rhythms; not only does the passage capture the tension of brave men, but the awesome power of the sea is summed up in that striking *land* image. It is their way of seeing this new element. As they fish, their minds are not always on the sea, but often filled with land memories, for this is the time of year when they would have worked in the shielings. Even in slight detail, Gunn sustains his land-sea contrast; their tackle is 'a crossbar of slim hazel . . . and a hook on a short horse-hair'. Ominous signs gather now. The boat is rotten; their buoy is made from the deliberately broken bagpipes of a dead piper. Tormad is sick; and they fail to recognise the 'ship with a light, like a small star', as not a morning star of hope but a navy vessel. They fail also to understand why the other herring boats are leaving so fast.

We are meant to feel anger towards the press-gang, and pity for Tormad — but something more. For Tormad *was* beginning to succeed as fisherman, *was* becoming the right man for the hour. Although Gunn does mean us to read that bitter remark 'they had learned that everything that spoke of power and wealth had to be feared' as part of an attack on authority and absentee landlords, and although the chapter ends with that pitiful and effective description of the sea glittering around one small derelict boat, there is something in the intimate way we have got to know Tormad which tells us that we are not done with him. The question is — why introduce us so completely to Tormad unless there is some meaning, which will illuminate the entire novel, to come from his death?

The important focus in this first part is on Catrine, women, and the land, and the beginning of her obsession, unhealthy and unbalanced, with land-security. We see this happening in Chapter One. Her humour and loyalty and love in the opening pages turns sour because she loves so fully, because she has seen the sea take her uncle. She has shared the poverty, the dysentery and colic that the displaced community has suffered. She naturally does not wish to lose all that she loves. Suddenly she changes, and Tormad knows that the change is far beyond her wayward moods: 'her eyes were suddenly those of an enemy, deliberately calculating, cold as greed'. She tries physically to restrain him. Even now, though, she doesn't completely break down, such is her courage, but in the end comes to the shore to see him off.

She has a long journey, literally and figuratively, ahead of her, which begins when she 'knows' that Tormad is dead. Her dreams told her, first prophesying evil befalling Tormad, and secondly bringing his wraith before her at the moment of his death.

The first dream's setting is not far from Kildonan church, the ancient cross cut in the rock, in the wood known as 'the wood of the Cell of Mary'. Catrine sees Tormad standing between two birch trees above a haunted pool, haunted by the spirit of a girl who has died of a broken heart. She is vividly conscious of Tormad and of the rowans 'heavy with clustered berries of a menacing blood-red'. Out of the wood comes a black horse. 'That's my horse,' says Tormad, Catrine in the dream is terrified, and will not ride the horse. He loosens her restraining hands and disappears on the horse sliding smoothly under the loch.

It is a haunting yet horrifying vision. It can be taken either as a supernatural glimpse into the future or as a psychological revelation. In this second light, its meaning is clear. Here are places holy to Catrine, Christian and pagan, with cross and ancient signs against evil, such as rowan and birch. Rowan is traditionally planted outside Highland cottages to ward off evil spirits. Catrine's community is 'on the wane', its ancient traditions warped by removal from origin. Her dream is thus set in autumn, the pool haunted by Catrine's fears of loss, holy images, and pagan signs now hostile. So the people of Dunster (with the exception of Catrine, Roddie and Finn) turn in superstitious fear against their most ancient holy places, like the House of Peace. It is a sign of the desolate times that symbols of peace and goodness, cross, rowan and birch, no longer have their traditional meaning, nor give protection in dream from the horse, which is the dreaded water-kelpie. Catrine's retreat prefigures a retreat of twenty years. But most crucial to the novel is the introduction of the rowan-blood motif, the outstanding image of land, past, and memory related to Catrine.

This was insinuated in Chapter One, with Catrine's mouth 'smiling and blood-red'. Already linked to Catrine are blood and rowan berry. As the images of spilled blood (in Tormad's boat, and in Horman's telling Catrine of it) accumulate, it becomes clear that in Catrine's mind the rowan berries *are* the badge of that blood, of Tormad's death:

> This pallor of living began in somewhere at the back of her mind to be blood-stained in the next two days. It was as though in dream, in another life, she heard the words: *Blood: rowan-red*. The words were soundless, a haunted rhythm, but their colour was bright as rowan berries or arterial blood.

The effects that Gunn will later achieve through this rowan imagery are astonishing. When Finn returns from a visit some seventeen years later to Dale with some rowan for his mother, time is short-circuited and Tormad's death and Catrine's agony are sharply brought before us. For the moment the meaning of this dream is that Catrine's deepest blood instincts are temporarily poisoned, and she turns against her home and herself. In this state she has her second dream, in which she sees Tormad dead, and in which, like Chris Guthrie accepting her dead Ewan back into her heart forever, she cries out to him with love. The difference between the situations is that Chris's experience brings reconciliation and peace, whereas Catrine's brings desolation and unrest so that she has, in the manner of the Ballads, to go 'into a Strange Country'.

Catrine's instincts, however poisoned, are at their well-springs good. 'She began to hate this place into which they had been driven; felt its dumb misery everywhere; but especially she feared and hated the sea.' She retreats, when crossing the moors, 'like the fox . . . a little hidden away herself from all she had been before', to curl up and sleep deep in the heather. Gunn links her with land, earth, growing things, and uses this to place her against the sea. How beautifully Gunn reveals Catrine's fearful mind in the piece of apparently simple narrative which follows!

A coast of precipices and wings and perilous depths. A coast of hard rock and sea. She turned her head to the heather moors that rose slowly inland, with the mountains behind. The mountains and the moors and the warm sun on them, brown and soft and playful. She kept towards the inside of the road, the cliffs and the sea like down-rushing dizzying wings in her breast.

When the road had left the cliffs and was wandering inland a little, she stopped. 'Now you have come far enough,' she said. 'I'll manage fine.'

The writing evokes her urge towards land-security. We are seeing through her eyes, just as later we will see through Finn's and occasionally Roddie's.

Again she dreams, of the horses of the Apocalypse, to waken to find that they are the stagecoach horses. Even with waking, though, these horses, a contact with the outside world (paralleled in Gibbon's *A Scots Quair* by the intrusion of motor cars into the ancient farming world), represent Authority, Worldly Powers which to a simple people mean repression and danger.

The land accepts Catrine to its bosom, and her quest lifts her steadily — until the intrusion of the shepherd. Having lost Tormad to a world of the alien power of men, she shuts herself off from the world of men. The shepherd represents that world. In addition, he is a lowlander, speaking broad Scots, representing the Highland Clearances, since he and dogs and sheep are what replaced the inland communities of the past.

Peace is at hand, however. Gunn introduces what is probably the most important single symbolic setting in the book, the House of Peace. Like Gibbon's Chris finding rest at her standing stones, Catrine finds the place, and the name sounding 'like a benediction . . . in her mind'. Roddie introduces her to the place, and takes her to Kirstie. Suddenly Catrine knows that an end has come to the vision of her running childhood that she now sees in her mind as if it were far outside. But she has one last ordeal to go through before she finds lasting peace. This is in the old man, Kirstie's father, reading the twenty-third psalm before bed. Its vital passages are those of the green pastures and the still waters. Not only are these the lines that Tormad and she had read the night before he went to

sea, the favourite lines of the children of the lost glens linke
always with the lost inland home, but they are also images sug
gesting a harmony in God's creation of water and earth, sea an
land. This harmony Catrine has lost:

> He maketh me to lie down in green pastures: he leadeth m
> beside the still waters. He restoreth my soul . . . Yea, though
> walk through the valley of the shadow of death.

This use of biblical imagery takes us out from Catrine to th
larger issues in which she is involved in this part. It is broadl
organised from her point of view, but the imagery also weaves itsel
around Roddie, Finn, and the Dunster community who have all t
learn to come to terms with the *wholeness* of God's created world
Land *and* Sea, crofting *and* fishing. What follows in the first par
relates now equally to the other two major protagonists of the book
Finn and Roddie. Gunn wants us to see them alongside Catrine
together with her immediate relatives, Kirstie, her father, and th
Dunster families who are also vital protagonists in the novel.

Thus Catrine is increasingly surrounded by other plots and foca
figures. Chapter Four, 'The First Hunt for The Silver Darlings'
leaves her temporarily to focus on Roddie. Chapter Five, 'Finn an
the Butterfly', moves to Finn as a child. Catrine isn't lost but im
plied, hovering just beyond them, repressing Finn's natural driv
towards the sea. Always the sea is her enemy, even the wind from
the sea, which tosses to ribbons Catrine's little ricks of hay
Catrine's coolness to Roddie stems from this hate, 'deep as an in
stinct', and when Finn begins his toddler's adventures Catrine'
reaction is to smother him with protection and love. An edge o
hysteria is always in Catrine, even at the hill market fair i
November, when Roddie, Finn and Don go off around the fai
without her. Finn's fun ends when Catrine finds him. Sh
reproaches Finn, while Don defends him *as a man* against women:

> 'Surely the poor fellow can have a drink with the rest. Eh
> Finn? Are you going home with your mother or are you stick
> ing by Roddie and me?'
> 'Come, Finn,' said Catrine.
> Finn hesitated . . . 'That's the boy! said Don. 'Away home

124

woman of the house, and leave the young man to enjoy
himself...'
'Come, Finn,' said Catrine firmly. She took his hand.
'Finn, Finn, my boy,' said Don, shaking his head, 'that's
what they do to you.'

This is followed by the more serious exchange with Finn when he
says he'll go to sea like Roddie, and Catrine vehemently forbids
him to think of the sea. He doesn't promise. It's significant that he
so definitely wants to go, and that he wants to sail his present, the
little boat. Chapter Eight sums up her feelings, in her fireside
reverie. She remembers the joy of possessing Finn as baby and
child, games safely played on the earth, in the trees and meadows.
'If she possessed nothing in the world but Finn, she had enough,
for ah! Finn was her own, her very own': but 'all that lovely time
was ending. For next summer Finn would be old enough to do the
herding himself, old enough to have his own ploys, to sail little
boats.' Catrine is too honest to hide for ever from the truths of life
or herself. She knows that 'little boats' will pose increasing sea-
challenges. The very song she sings, 'Hó-van, hó-van, Gorry óg O',
is all about the loss of the child by the mother — and the song is
crucial in the book, for Finn, much later. In the long run she does
have the rare courage to respond to Kirstie's warning. Kirstie's
finest gift to Catrine and to Finn is her liberating plea to Catrine
from her plague-agony:

'You'll never keep that boy from the sea. If you wish him
well, don't try.'
Catrine was silent.
Kirstie turned her eyes. 'You are still against him?'
'I do not want him to go to sea.'
'More ugly deaths on this land now than ever on sea. If you
put the boy against his nature, you'll warp him. Remember
that.'
Catrine bowed her head.

That bowing is symbolic and important. It marks Catrine's turning point in her dealings with Finn. Catrine now reads to dying
Kirstie the twenty-third psalm. Green pastures and still waters

125

begin to come together for Catrine. She has turned an important corner. She sees that death is no prerogative of the sea, taking as it does so many of Dunster's land-folk, and that it is her own Finn who gives her life back by bringing her medicines from Wick, after his heroic walk (his first manly deed). In Parts Two and Three, her struggle is that of coming to terms with her love for living Roddie and dead Tormad.

Why does Gunn not simply and cleanly show Tormad's son achieving what his father failed to do? First, the story is not just Finn's, it's Catrine's, and the community's, showing how it receives and heals its sick. Roddie is part of that healing community. Roddie exists as necessary father figure to Finn, pulling him towards the sea, away from women and crofts, to the world of comradeship of men. Finally he becomes Finn's rival, the figure of heroism against whom Finn has to measure himself. Without Roddie the novel would not have had that sense of cyclic repetition, of Tormad-Roddie-Finn as waves, life moving ever onwards. Roddie is Sea and Man against Catrine as Land and Woman. It is like Jason and his Argonauts or the great heroes of Icelandic saga; he goes in quest not of Golden Fleeces, but Silver Darlings. Where Tormad was conceived in human and limited terms, clumsy in his sea-dealings, Roddie is utterly different, fanatical in his dedication to the sea, fair where Tormad was dark, the youngest skipper in Dunster, the archetype of the new herring industry. His colossal strength is constantly stressed — 'the mad Viking' famed for his great skill as a fisherman. Indeed Special Hendry is scornful of small ventures like Tormad's in the face of the greater ventures to come, in which Roddie is seen as 'the coming generation'. In these 'fabulous days' Roddie is already part of fable. What Gunn will show through Roddie is that this apparent heroic nature is only one side of a larger whole. Roddie himself was only 'married to the sea' (as he told his fellow-fishermen at the beginning of Chapter Seven) because Catrine was unavailable, and his great achievements at sea, though undoubtedly heroic, are pointless unless married to community and family. This is the major theme of the book, and emerges most clearly in Part Three with Finn.

But before we deal with Finn there is another 'protagonist', an entity of supreme importance for Gunn: Community, with its racial tradition behind it. Like Catrine, Roddie, and Finn, all the communities of the north-east are to be seen in Part One as in a state of change painfully forgetting their old way of life in their crofts in the upland straths. Added to this is their bewilderment at the new evangelism which told them that the Clearances were brought upon them for their sins. Throughout the book we see that this separation from their past has damaged them. From the piper of Chapter One who destroyed his pipes and cursed the Countess of Sutherland, to the fear that Catrine develops for traditional emblems of peace and blessedness, from the fear of the Dunster people of the House of Peace to the North Uist people's complaint that the old dances are dying out, stopped by the new ministers, we realise that transition is adversely affecting many communities. Yet these communities (unlike Gibbon and his) confront tragedies with quiet, understated solidarity. There is no more moving part of the novel than when the Dale men and Tormad's father go over to Helmsdale to pick up the derelict boat:

> Then the Dale men came over. Tormad's father went to Murray and asked him about the meaning of what had happened in a quiet voice. No anger, no bluster; a nod now and then, and the eyes staring away through grey screens. What he wanted to know was how long they would keep him. 'It's difficult to say,' Murray answered. 'But it'll be a year or two anyway, I'm feared . . . ' 'What is the longest time you have known of anyone?' 'Oh, I have known men nearly twenty years in it, but they came out at the end well and strong and with a pension. Some men like it . . . ' 'Twenty years,' repeated Tormad's father, looking beyond his own death. 'Ah, well,' he added quietly, 'I'll be getting back. It's hard on them at home. He has a young wife.'

Understatement here is more effective than a more dramatic presentation.

Some critics have accused Gunn of painting his characters too 'white' and too similar. Gunn specifically emphasises the fact that his communities *were* similar, and 'good', because they belonged to a tradition of Gaelic community. The varied characters of the *Seafoam*, or the later crew of Finn's voyage to North Uist, are subtly humorous and credibly different throughout the novel. Long-standing jokes are carried on, without being laboured, over years — like Callum teasing Rob about his widow in Stornoway, or Rob baiting Callum about the whale. Community humour is sly and allusive, but rarely bitter and deeply hurtful; in tragedy, aware of vulnerable areas just as Roddie, on meeting Catrine for the first time, instinctively knows that she has lost relatives in the press-gang incident, and leaves the issue alone, or when Kirstie's father draws the poison from her in his wise blessing at the end of Chapter Three.

Kirstie's father has an importance far beyond the small amount of space he is allowed in the book. Like so many of Gunn's Old Men, from Hector of *Young Art and Old Hector* to the three old story tellers who impress Finn so much in North Uist, at the end of the novel, he is archetypal, representing accumulated wisdom and goodness. Although he and Finn never meet, there is a link between them; for Gunn has Finn born exactly as the old man dies, to tell us that life arises out of the shadow of death (another reading of the twenty-third psalm!). As Gaelic tradition has it, the soul or life-force of the old man is passed on to Finn. From such as the old man Finn will inherit social grace, feeling for others, moral values and tradition.

The full importance of the role of such people and of community will emerge in North Uist later. What we need to understand here is that Gunn (like Gibbon) uses the concept of 'the collective unconscious' throughout this and many of his novels. The 'collective unconscious' in Gunn's communities and individuals is that deep racial memory and instinctive knowledge of tradition which Gunn sees as accumulating through thousands of years, without being taught or learned, in the individual mind. It is 'collective' because it has been 'collected' by the race, so that, for example, young Kenn in *Highland River* knew without being told how to tackle his first salmon in the Well pool. It's 'unconscious' because it only emerges into consciousness at moments of stress — otherwise the knowledge is dormant. At times this mysterious operation of the mind can seem supernatural, as when Finn 'sees' the priest in the House of Peace.

Gunn's use of this kind of supernatural experience, alongside his use of the traditional supernatural (such as Catrine 'seeing' Tormad when he died), is rich but sometimes puzzling, in the sense that we wonder whether he means us to take a psychological interpretation

128

or accept that we are witnessing the supernatural. For example — are we to read Catrine's dream of the rowans and water horse as 'second sight' or simply as the nightmare of a worried person fearing the worst? Does she really see Tormad after his death? Was Finn dreaming when he 'saw' the priest?

Frequently Gunn emphasises modes of perception which aren't rational. When the shepherd followed Catrine, 'for a moment she *felt* blind physical forces balancing behind her'. She 'feels' the power of the House of Peace. Both Catrine and Una have moments when, sitting inside a house at night, they 'see' (when they really couldn't see) Roddie and Finn outside. Finn 'feels' the presence of someone like the Druid in the little cell at the top of the Cliff of the Seven Hunters.

I suggest that Gunn creates a 'take-it-or-leave-it' situation, because he himself is both traditional Gael and modern rationalist, aware of complexities of psychology. We can read it at whichever level we wish — at the psychological or the supernatural — or even a kind of intermingling of both.

Similarly he allows Christian imagery and pagan tradition to sit together. Is he Christian or pagan? There are Christian images which 'work' for Catrine and Finn, in the twenty-third psalm, in the House of Peace. Christian references are important, such as the references to the walls of Jericho, or the blessings of the old man. But alongside these are pagan rituals, like Roddie's 'neidfire' to boil the water to 'sain' the beasts, or the 'Cold Iron!' cry whenever God's name is mentioned on board boat, or the tribute in fish that is paid to the witch Lexie.

Gunn makes no selection of any creed, faith or legend as having a monopoly of truth, whether it be Christianity (Sandy Ware's evangelical brand, Kirstie's more practical, her father's deep piety) or pagan tradition or legend. He shows that 'feyness', fatalistic acceptance of imminent death, need not in fact lead to death. Gunn accepts a central mystery, which he calls 'God'. Below this, however, Gunn allows an immense range of symbols and metaphors, his sole criterion for validity, Christian or pagan, being that they show vitality and beauty. All have emerged from time as ways of saying something which generations have found significant.

Here Gunn shares Gibbon's attitudes to the past. The ancient Golden Age of the Elder People is remembered through these traditions, legends and rituals. As in Gibbon's treatment, modern displaced man may have lost some contact with his roots. Nevertheless, the novel places these vital memories of a clean, pagan-and-Christian ancient way of life *against* what is corrupting it, like Sandy Ware's poisoned version of Christianity, absentee land-owners, and powers that send press-gangs and break the traditional spirit of the people. The communities of the north-east have learned bitterly to distrust all that is outside (which includes gamekeepers and lowland shepherds). Church and landowner have failed their people. But Gunn is not, as Gibbon was, against all property-owning capitalism and all religion. His treatment of 'Special' Hendry demonstrates that he allows that private enterprise may often benefit society generally. Hendry is a good man.

This background lies behind Finn, the central character of the book, who is born into a 'fabulous' time, with tradition and legend — and psychological strain — surrounding him. Finn's development in the book is dual. It is a private development, a search for 'self' comparable to Wordsworth's in *The Prelude*, with Gunn showing Finn's need to draw a 'circle' round himself so that he is his own man — not Catrine's, nor enslaved to his love for Una. Finn learns the paradox that true discovery of private self can only be made when one is reconciled in harmony with family and community. These discoveries are shown in the book in stages, similar to the stages used by James Joyce in his presentation of Stephen Daedalus in *A Portrait of the Artist as a Young Man*. Wordsworth referred to similar moments of discovery as 'timeless moments'. Joyce called them 'epiphanies', that is, experiences of intense spiritual significance. They are fundamental to Finn's development, together with their most important locale, that outstanding symbol of the novel, the House of Peace.

Gunn's fiction is ultimately concerned with 'the other landscape'. The second part of his fictional career, from *The Silver Darlings* on, was taken up with exploring a 'fourth dimension', an area of mystery beyond the rational and obviously human, beyond our space and time. To this extent he was always a 'religious' and sometimes a 'mystical' writer. *The Silver Darlings* balances Finn's very real quest for self-knowledge with his discovery that this world has within it hints of a timeless harmony, a supra-human state of delight, peace, and wholeness. The vision is reminiscent of Wordsworth and 'Tintern Abbey', 'Intimations of Immortality' and *The Prelude*, and Gunn has admitted his great debt to the poet. Gunn explores a wider field than Wordsworth, since Finn's epiphanies not only suggest 'the other landscape' but link him also with his ancestors and his community. Where Wordsworth's experience was private, Finn's is social as well. And it is the House of Peace which gives Finn his deepest spiritual experiences. It is the symbol of Gaelic and Celtic *living* tradition, for all that some of the people will not listen to its message.

The House of Peace is Finn's symbol. As he is also meant as a kind of reincarnation of the great hero of the Irish and Scottish sagas, the mythical and legendary cycle of stories concerning 'the Fianns', it is important to see him always in connection with it. It is *his* circle in so many ways, a gateway through time, linking him with the mysterious ancient leader, Finn MacCoul. We feel its radiating influence for Good and spiritual revival, just as we feel the more desolate and elegiac influence of Gibbon's standing stones in *Sunset Song*. Let us look at the growth of Finn, real boy and mythical reincarnation in part one. Why does Gunn introduce us — quite suddenly — to Finn as a young child, in Chapter Five, 'Finn and the Butterfly'? Surely because Finn's adventure with the butterfly is specially significant, something of crucial importance has happened for the first time to the boy. There is humour and charm in Gunn's picture of the childish fears and guilts, and strange, circumscribed world of the toddler's vision. Alongside this runs a poetic symbolism which shows that the boy has discovered a mysterious *moral* world. Already Finn is seen as venturesome for his age, straining against his mother's smothering love. This episode is a microcosm of all that will happen to him, an anticipatory parallel to later life. The movement instinctively to water, and the brown trout, is the movement of his life, to sea and fish. He conquers his fear, for even as he cries for his mother to help him over the river-boulders, he has taken the step of courage forward, to discover his *self*, even though he does immediately after fall on his bottom in the water.

Most important is his discovery of guilt. Finn, by killing the butterfly discovers sin and death. It is his first moral act. This sequence is very Wordsworthian, reminding of *The Prelude* scene when, to the guilty boy, all nature seemed to disapprove and mountains threatened angrily. Finn is disobeying his mother's orders to stay close to the croft, fascinated by the dancing butterfly:

> The butterfly rose and danced on through the air, down the burnside.
>
> He followed it at once, without thought, because he had had by the pool for a moment a queer dread that his mother's head and shoulders would rise large and menacing over the edge of the brae . . .
>
> There was something in this wood a little bit like what there was in the butterfly, only it was very much stronger than the butterfly. Now and then the wood was like a thing whose heart had stopped, watching.

Finn kills the butterfly, and suddenly is on his own, a separate human being. That is why the chapter is so named, and why such play is made on the name of the creature in Gaelic. Finn is desperately upset to think that he has killed 'God's fool', the ancient name Roddie gave it, preferring the other name 'the grey fool' because then the butterfly isn't God's, but just any old butterfly, without any moral importance. This microcosmic chapter ends with Finn asleep in the circle of the House of Peace, where he'll be found at the very end of the novel. For the first of many times it offers him refuge and sympathy.

To bring Finn on at the age of four enables Gunn to show the boy as a barrier between Roddie and Catrine, as in their quarrel about Roddie taking Finn out in his boat. To show Finn as a baby would have been irrelevant, although it's not so to describe his birth later on. And even though this chapter is followed by the chapter 'Land and Sea' which is about Roddie and fishing and Catrine and crofting, it still relates to Finn since it shows us the opposed forces in his life. Gunn interweaves like this all the time — so that, for example, even in a 'Finn' chapter like 'Finn Blows his Trumpet', the beginning is about Roddie being married to the sea, at the height of his powers, which brings out once again the cyclic theme of the novel; as Roddie rises to his heroic feats, Finn enters the world of men.

Finn moves on to the second stage of his development. Significantly Roddie shows him how to blow his trumpet, in the sense of 'blowing one's own trumpet', asserting one's own self.

This first blast signals to the world that Finn has arrived. We see too his fearful desire that Roddie, his unofficial father, should show his strength by ringing the bell, and we've seen how Catrine drags him away from this bold new world of men. All this comes together at the end of the chapter, 'The Spirit and the Flesh', when, after a harrowing session with Black Sandy Ware, filled with images of Jericho and Moses, he has his vivid dream of the Wall:

> Down where the burns joined, there was a drystone dyke taller than himself. He had climbed it once, but the stones on the top were shaky and he had got a fright. If one of the stones fell on you it would kill you! Well, he had seen this wall in his dream, but it was a much bigger wall, though it was the same wall, too. Now there was something about this wall that had always seemed to threaten him, to dare him and yet to threaten him, with a queer sort of expression on its face formed by the curious shapes of the holes between the stones. The wall had to be tumbled down for it was a bad wall. 'Go forward and sound the trumpet!' cried a great man behind him, who was Moses, though he looked like Sandy Ware. There were many people behind, as Finn went forward. The trumpet hung from the branch of a tree, as Finn had sometimes hung his own trumpet, but this was a much bigger trumpet than Finn's, and not straight but curved like one of the great horns on a Highland cow. Both the wall and the trumpet grew bigger as he drew near. But he took the mouthpiece in his lips and blew all the breath that was in him. The trumpet roared like a bull, and at that one or two of the stones on top started to shake; then the wall began to sway; he turned and ran as the wall fell, but the stones came after him, leaping over the grass, and he stumbled, and the stones leaped on to his legs.

The wall is his mother's confining love, but it is also the wall confining his people, which he and Roddie will push down through their sea-exploits. It is a wall of restricting ideas too, which is why Sandy Ware is there in the dream, and why the Jericho memory inserts itself. The fear of the wall is the projection of childhood fear, giving the wall a threatening face. But then the symbolism moves on to the level of myth, and an eerie music comes in. The trumpet has become the great curved horn of Finn MacCoul, and Gunn's Gaelic readers would immediately recognise the meaning, that the great heroes, the Fianns, are slumbering in their mountain halls, awaiting the call on Finn MacCoul's trumpet which will rouse them to life, to aid mankind in its eternal battle against evil. Finn in the dream asserts his courage and blows this great trumpet — and not only are we to see this as a summoning of Finn MacCoul, we are to see Finn *becoming* Finn MacCoul as well. But Finn is not quite ready yet, and in the dream the stones leap on him.

By Chapter Nine, 'The Seashore', Finn has changed. His dog has the name Oscar (a later dog is Bran) — the names of Finn MacCoul's great wardogs. Finn now *is* a hunter, aged 13. He snares rabbits but is impatient with land hunting, drawn elsewhere, just as he was drawn by the butterfly:

> 'The Sea! the sea! the boats coming in! The lightness and brightness of the sea, and boats, and fishing, and fun!'

Again he is disobeying his mother. The flounder they catch is 'the real fish of the deep sea, such as the winter boats caught far off the land' — it's obvious where Finn now wants to be! 'They forgot about time, crofts, cows' — that is, they forget the Land. Then follows the struggle, so close to that of Kenn and the salmon in *Highland River*, with the eel which is 'the father of all serpents'. Finn in disobeying his mother is guilty, and the serpent is the temptation which keeps him at the shore. But Gunn uses the serpent in two senses, just as in his novel *The Serpent* he uses the Christian sense as well as the deeper pagan sense. In Celtic lore the serpent is symbol of the earth spirit and wisdom, an older meaning by far than the relatively recent Christian symbol of evil. Gunn uses both together here. The serpent is an emblem of Finn's wrong doing, but Finn has to pit his instincts, like Kenn, against his opponent, to find out about his own resources of courage and skill. He is indeed learning a kind of wisdom, and on this level the serpent becomes the emblem of that deeper need to disobey in order to develop. Again, there is the sting in the tail, for he fails temporarily. Typically, Finn takes his wounded self for healing to the House of Peace, while Kirstie smiles to herself and takes his side against Catrine. 'The man was stirring!' she thinks. And he hasn't lost totally in his battle with Catrine (or 'anyone'!):

> He had got through it much better than he had expected — because he had got through it intact. He was whole, and if his mind was dark it had a queer smile in it, bitter a little, but still his own... The monstrous eel came out of the forest of seaweed... he had held on! He hadn't let go... If anyone tried to keep you back, to keep you shut in a croft — you could go away and sail over the seven seas to strange lands, and so be free in yourself...
>
> His mother moved restlessly in her bed, and at once his mind gave a whirl like a caught eel.

Finn is now 'on the seashore' of his own life. Now he sees Roddie and his mother, at 38 and 33 as 'old people'. Finn will learn to change despite himself, and through the help of an agency which builds up its stature through the book to emerge triumphantly at the end as the distilled meaning of the entire account. The importance of song and story to Finn and to the book cannot be over-stressed. It is the way that Finn sees meaning given to the cyclic experiences of birth, discovery of self, and death. Finn will at critical points in his life realise truth through the medium of a story or song and sometimes through giving his own experience form through controlling it in his own storytelling. As yet, however, Finn only grasps that song can move him at times unbearably, as at old Lachlan's house:

> As they approached the house, they heard singing. Involuntarily, Finn paused, and the rhythm went all through the night, over the land, and quivered in his heart... the rhythm of the song was more intimate to him than his own face... when all the voices surged together, rising, his body quivered as if sluiced in cold water.
>
> Anna's voice had made him think of his own mother.
>
> Life in the dim night, under the stars, over the land, the old, old land, the curved thatch, the still birch trees, the surge of the singing, rising as smoke rises from a fire,

spreading out over the immemorial land, under the dying moon.

Throughout the novel, songs of this nature (whether sung as lullaby by Catrine to Finn, or here, or by the girls of Lewis or North Uist) will call deeply to Finn, reminding him of his part in his race. He cannot escape the song of life, even though temporarily as now he struggles to avoid it, by leaving Lachlan's. His anguish takes him to his House of Peace.

The House of Peace gives Finn the strangest experience of his life shortly after this. He has been to Dale to avoid illness at home. On his return Kirstie is ill, he is forced away from his mother, and in great misery he goes to his Circle, and sleeps:

> Now, as he fell asleep, he dreamed, though never in after life could he quite satisfy himself that it was really sleep and a dream, for everything about him was exactly the same, the trees, the situation and the evening light; it was the same moment; and yet like that instant which had preceded the coming of the known world when he was a little boy, so now he seemed to be awake when he saw standing by the near cell the tall figure of an old man in a white cape with the front part of his head quite bald. The face was extremely distinct, and though it had the dignity of Roddie's father in its expression, the face itself was one he had never seen before. The face did not speak to him or move; it just looked, the body standing still in a natural way.
>
> But the look was extraordinarily full of understanding, and somewhere in it there was a faint humour, the humour that knows and appreciates and yet would not smile to hurt, yet the smile was there. It knew all about Finn, and told him nothing — not out of compassion, but not of needlessness.
>
> As Finn's eyes opened wider, the figure faded.

Yet again Gunn presents one of these 'timeless moments' into the vision of the 'fourth dimension' which hovers always a little beyond Finn. We can read this psychologically. Stress has given him hallucinations, understandably linked with the person of Roddie, since the 'old monk' looks like Roddie's father. The dream purges Finn of accumulated tension. But how would Finn know of the ancient Celtic Christian habit of shaving the head differently from later Christian monks? Possibly through legend and story? Whether we read this rationally or supernaturally, however, the symbolism is clear. Finn is admitted to the past. He is one of the Elder People, and shortly after joins Roddie (since he cannot join his mother) in 'the new life, the life of men'. As he walks by the river, the House of Peace is strong in his mind, 'very old inside him, older than peat-smoke', and a new awareness of symbol and ritual is given to him. Thinking of the rituals he's just witnessed, like 'saining' the beasts, Finn asks Roddie, and Roddie simply answers — 'Why do we do many a thing?' Finn thinks:

> A strange world indeed, older than the House of Peace, old as the legendary salmon of knowledge that lay in the pool under the hazelnuts of wisdom, and perhaps older than that, with more mysterious things in it than the mind dreamt of. And how rich the thought of that invisible complexity was on a sunny, wind-bright morning! Everything, even the grey stones, with a hidden life!

We should set this redeeming vision of river, holy place, salmon of knowledge and hazelnuts of wisdom against Catrine's warped vision at the beginning of the novel of dark pool, a holy place which has lost its helping power, water kelpie, and rowan berries which have become images of blood and death; Life against Death; Light against Darkness. Finn's mind at the shore is filled with light and delight but we should also remember that the Dunster folk (with the exception of Roddie) fear the House of Peace and its ghostly monk, its fairy music, its headless horseman. Black Sandy has turned them against their heritage, and 'Peace' has become unrest. It is the measure of Finn's progress that he conquers such fears.

This first part of the novel ends with Finn going on the journey to Wick to find another kind of practical, scientific knowledge — the cure for his mother. Again he passes a test. By giving his mother Life, Finn releases himself.

A new effect is achieved in the second and third parts. Gunn is able to show events as cyclic, history echoing itself. Although Roddie's controlled and skilful departure does not repeat Tormad's mistakes, it reminds us of Tormad. The reminder is deliberate, with the time past-time present juxtaposition of the appearance of Ronnie, who went to sea with Tormad, with the *Seafoam* moving out on her epic voyage. We don't hear his story yet, since we are at sea, away from Land and Women, in the camaraderie of men. This comradeship is, however, a form of retreat, an over-emphasis of the values and pleasures of escape from Land. The running metaphor for this 'enchanted' period is that of the boat — and crew — in a wooden dream, sealed off from contact and responsibility other than with and to each other.

Although the emphasis is now on Sea and Men, the opposing Land-and-Women imagery is sustained cleverly by the devices of recollection and representation throughout part two. In conversation, the crew reflect upon the land and its claims. In the Flannan Isles or Lewis, similar land and community problems represent the problems the crew have left behind. Rob's stories of landlords and rackrents keep the land in mind, though now sea represents release:

> Pleasant it was to see the land slipping by . . . like a gate closing in a dream until all their kindred were shut off, leaving them to adventure . . . still was the land, and somehow a little sad, held to its own dream, and never able to move . . .
>
> This is what Catrine could not understand — this fellowship of men. Who would barter it for intrigue and miserliness and cruelty and law-suits and manses?

And Finn frequently remembers the House of Peace, so that it is not lost to him as an inspiring force.

But Gunn cannot rely completely on recollection to keep alive Catrine and Una as pressures on Finn. This explains the strange set of circumstances at Loch Luirbost, when, after the fight in the Stornoway inn, Finn goes with Seumus and stays the night with Alan and his sisters. The events remind us of Finn's resentment of his mother and attraction to Una. Alan is Finn, older, more enmeshed, because Lewis, now in the grip of an even stronger religious revival than that of Sandy Ware in Dunster, has caught Alan in a trap where his sexual and emotional instincts are repressed by his sisters, driving him to the only release possible, that of drink. Unusually wild, Finn nevertheless feels for Alan:

138

And all at once he saw Alan caught in the tendrils of their mercy, as the sheep of sacrifice was caught in the thicket. It was a queer, stark, dreadful vision.

Roddie — Roddie — caught in the thorns, too. Years, upon years, upon years.

All women seem to Finn now to be snares, stopping the hero from his adventures. This part asserts defiantly the importance of the heroic quest.

There is much of the saga in these pages. The bond of men is stressed, and their Norse stoicism. They are 'seamen who could not be beaten down, seamen who went quiet and steady when death, the omnipresent of the dark ones, felt he could engulf them at last'. They even have a kind of communication that is non-verbal:

> He had waited for talk, for expressions of opinion, however casual . . . There had been none. All at once they were preparing to shoot [put out nets], as if some silent common intelligence had been at work.

An explicit parallel with heroic achievements of the past is brought about through chapter titles ('Storm and Precipice', 'The Golden Cask', reminding of Jason and his Argonauts seeking the Golden Fleece) and the flavour of names and places. Thurso is now seen as 'Thor's Town'; the Orkneys are 'fabulous'; Finn climbs the Cliff of the Seven Hunters; the prow is 'the school-book illustration of the Viking Longship, with its high carven head'. He suddenly knows 'the impulse that in the beginning moved these great wanderers of the sea . . .' The voyage is full of legends and land disaster, like the tale of the Rona islanders who were destroyed by rats. All these events are enjoyed by the crew in a Viking spirit of understated humour and loyalty. They are, in their incredible voyage which takes them in an open boat far out into the Atlantic, creating their own myth, as the Stornoway curer states when they go off yet again to fish when others stay at home. 'Why didn't they wait until the morning?' asks one. 'Because,' answers Bain, 'that's what's going to conquer the sea.'

Throughout, Roddie is the Viking leader, rock-steady at the helm, assured and courageous, the incarnation of the ocean itself.

He even becomes the 'berserker', the superhuman mad Viking, on shore, after the dogfish have ruined his nets. Curiously, on shore Roddie is much less happy — as when he loses the initiative to Finn at the Cliffs of the Seven Hunters.

But under the surface of this enchanted sea lurks the dogfish — and in a brilliant shift of image and meaning, Gunn applies the notion to the sea of Roddie's mind, with its 'dogfish swirl' (the pent-up poison of his memory of Catrine) which is released by Big Angus's baiting:

> It was as if the dogfish were everywhere . . . things were brewing in Roddie; working to a head. Instead of being proud, as he might be, at having brought his boat through the storm on the west side, Finn knew perfectly well that he was touchy about it . . . those black unfathomable moments between Roddie and himself at the Seven Hunters. Deep down, like a poison.

The tension between them manifests itself increasingly as a desire on Finn's part to do deeds (like climbing the Seven Hunters) which Roddie couldn't do (even at the risk of being irresponsible, which Finn is when he cavorts with the sheep on the cliff-top). We see more clearly than confused Finn what's going on, that he is becoming separate, becoming his own self — but, like Roddie, he also exists on the mythical level.

Finn is the mascot of the boat, with the best eyesight, the ability to 'whistle' up the wind, the luck to hear in Loch Luirbost of the whereabouts of the Silver Darlings. His cliff climb translates him for a moment into a real hero, 'laughing like an immortal youth' from the top. This climb becomes the material of legend. And what does Finn find when he climbs his cliff but the presence of the House of Peace yet again? In the ancient monastic cell 'Finn felt that he was not alone'. Finn says later:

> 'I felt as if someone invisible had just left and was maybe coming back. I felt he was an old quiet man. I was a little afraid and yet not afraid. But I have had that feeling at home.'

Finn has discovered that his own problems are to be found in varied forms — in Alan, for example; that the sea has its own equivalent of the plague in the dogfish. What he has not yet discovered is that Una is a vital part of his maturation, that Roddie must marry Catrine, and that he has been as unbalanced and obsessive about the sea throughout this voyage as Catrine ever was about the land. It remains to the third movement to resolve, suddenly and majestically, Finn's doubts and confusions. But he has done what his father set out to do.

Part Three is dominated by the image of the circle, turning (like the Celtic serpent of wisdom, with its tail in its mouth) back upon the book's beginning.

We go back in Chapter Nineteen, 'Sea Love', to meet Ronnie, whom we left at the opening of Part Two surprising Catrine. We hear the details of Tormad's death, but although this reminds us of Tormad's bravery, Ronnie's function is that of contrast to Finn and Roddie. In the cycle of life Gunn accepts that some 'go under'. Ronnie is such. That is why Gunn stresses his spent quality, his faded, passive cleanness, like bleached driftwood. His discussion with Finn when Finn visits Dale again after his voyage is important, for Catrine as well as Finn. Finn can accept now a picture of his picture, a living and noble memory. More important is Ronnie's argument against his own world-wide voyaging:

> 'They were telling me of your story of adventure into the Western Ocean.'
> 'That was nothing.'
> 'It took you to the edge of death — and further than that no adventure can travel in this life.'
> 'Oh, I don't know,' said Finn, feeling restless.
> 'I know,' said Ronnie. And he added, with a quiet finality in his voice . . .
> 'We were driven: you went.'

That is Ronnie's failure. He has chosen to live by the outside world's rules. That is why Catrine cannot entertain his proposal of marriage. She, for all her illness, has come through alive and part of Dunster, whereas Ronnie will till his death be the returned exile. Catrine's final vision of him shows his role:

She would never get away from the past with Ronnie. He was its ghost. The strath, the outline of the hills, Tormad, the red berries.

Ronnie's last usefulness is precisely because he is a ghost. He can lay the past, and this is done with a terrible beauty in the suggestion to Finn that he take the rowan berries to Catrine to remind her of her strath. The blood-red berries have been used as motif throughout to show Catrine's fixed idea of Tormad, her past violently murdered. How moving it is that Finn should be the agent of her release from this twenty-year-old nightmare! She cannot pretend that Tormad is alive. She gives in to Roddie, and is cruelly torn between Finn and Roddie. Finn's petulant gift of the berries causes her to collapse. After this she is changed, reborn:

> But behind this emotion her mind was gathering its cunning, which knew neither shame nor bitterness, only the real knowledge of life as it was, of the day as it came. And for the first time she felt in touch with Roddie's inner mind.

The berries cannot darken her mind any longer. She is now prepared, sadly, to let Finn go his own completely separate way, recognising his fate. Her life has turned full circle.

Roddie's life turns too. He becomes Land-and-Sea based, balanced now between elements. If Finn could only see it, he is now the old Roddie, imitated by the boys of the village as he used to imitate Roddie (he hears that one boy has fallen off a cliff copying Finn's Seven Hunters climb!). He even strikes his friend in the pub as Roddie struck him and 'sees' Una in the strange fashion that Roddie 'saw' Catrine. On the mythical plane he moves even close to complete identification with Finn MacCoul. The old drover of Dale sees 'a vision — of the youth of Finn MacCoul himself', asking 'Are the days of Finn MacCoul coming back upon us?'

Paradoxically, the closer Finn gets to the centre of his own circle of self, community, tradition, the further he seems in some ways to be from it. He is estranged from his mother, from Roddie, and almost loses Una. But this is the lull before the spiritual storm which brings Finn to wholeness.

First, though, there is a real storm which makes several things clearer to Finn. It is an echo of Tormad's disaster, but out of it Finn rediscovers union with Roddie. In stress he finds that he and Roddie are still a heroic pair, and that the old camaraderie is there till death. The rescue is land-based, so that from the land he and Roddie save friends from the sea. Women play the role here of ultimate life-givers, for when Roddie has failed to revive the drowned fisherman it is the mother who opens her garments and places the boy's feet on her breast to give human warmth. Here Finn sees a whole community in concerted action, each part helping each, land and sea locked in an eternal juxtaposition.

The last voyage sums up all previous movements outwards. Again the boat goes by Loch Eriboll and the Orkneys, although this time, on Finn's suggestion, they go even further and catch more fish. The passages at North Uist are meant to bring Tir-Nan-Og, the 'Green Isle of the Great Deep', the Celtic paradise, into our minds, for here are unspoiled, innocent Elder People who have much to teach Finn. They are meant to represent what Finn's own people must have been like before their Clearance, because in their hospitable, humorous lifestyle they resemble the community of *Butcher's Broom*:

> The nights they spent in that remote place were never to be forgotten by Finn. They had the influence on his life of a rare memory that would come and go by the opening of a small window far back in his mind. Through such an opening a man may see a sunny, green place . . . at once far back in the mind.

This imagery echoes that of Finn's perception of 'the other landscape', of that other dimension to life which Finn glimpses. 'There were moments . . . when to Finn it seemed a forgotten place that had lived on.' And there is a strange connection between Finn and the storytellers of the district, especially one of the three:

> for the old man's first name was the same as Finn's, which was likewise Finn MacCoul's, the great hero of the noble Fianns, whose marvellous exploits were this storyteller's province.

143

It is this old man who commends Finn for his storytelling:

> Old Finn-son-of-Angus said to him: 'You told the story well. You brought us into the far deeps of the sea and we were lost with you in the Beyond where no land is, only wind and wave and the howling of the darkness. You kept us in suspense on the cliffs, and you had some art in the way you referred to our familiars of the other world before you told of the figure of the man you felt by the little stone house. There you saw no one and you were anxious to make this clear, smiling at your fancy. It was well enough done. It was done, too, with the humour that is the play of drift on the wave. And you were modest. Yet — all that is only a little — you had something more, my hero, something you will not know — until you look at it through your eyes, when they are old as mine.'
>
> 'What do you mean by that?' asked Finn.
>
> But the old man shook his head and turned away. 'Go to your sleep, my boy. Many a one may come,' he muttered to himself, 'in the guise of the stranger.'

The third night begins with Hector asking about the Dunster folk and their dances, and marvelling that they have not heard of 'the real ancient dances like... The Fight of the Cocks' and the like. With the telling remark that the new ministers are stamping out these dances, Hector shows Finn The Old Wife of the Mill-dust. The dance describes a fair girl and a dark man; the killing of the girl; the sorrow of the man; the ritual of regeneration, and the final rebirth by touching her heart with the Druid's wand. They dance with vigorous happiness. The meaning for Finn is that out of death must come life; that his mother must have her new life.

Then after a passing but significant reference to the golden butterfly that is man's soul ('if you catch that butterfly and kill it you kill the soul of man in its fight. Like God's fool, it flits'), Finn is transported back to childhood and his mother with the lullaby sung by Matili, which is the song his mother sang to him:

> At first it was the mother and child in communion, but, as the rhythm went on, the mother's face lifted from her child and stared away over the green braes and over the burn. And

the child felt this withdrawnness in the mother and felt it too in himself, yet could neither protest nor move, held by the song's intangible loveliness with the half-terrifying, sweet sadness at its core. And the child was apart from the mother, and the mother from the child, though he was sitting on her lap, close, close to her.

The effect upon Finn was deep and self-revealing. Love for his mother cried out in him, the love that now understood the withdrawn fatality of the mother. He had been blind, blind. The awful inexorable implicity of the singing became too much to bear. He tried to put it from him, not to listen; he moved his head and pressed his right heel into the clay floor, so that his body be kept within control. He wanted to cry out, for the relief of the cry. They were all so still, listening to the girl singing the old lullaby of the mother whose child was stolen by the fairies:

> I left my darling lying here,
> A-lying here, a-lying here,
> I left my darling lying here,
> To go and gather blaeberries.

> Hó-van, hó-van, Gorry óg O,
> Gorry óg O, Gorry óg O;
> Hó-van, hó-van, Gorry óg O,
> I've lost my darling baby, O!

Finn has gained all the experience necessary to transform his life. By singing his own song, 'As the Rose Grows Merry in Time', he contributes towards the transmission of values and culture and tradition through song and story. This is the song of life too; and Finn's singing of the tasks that must be faced by the young hero is nothing less than a song of self-recognition. He has been setting himself tasks which he must perform before he is fit to take Una. The tasks of the song ('An acre of land you must plough unto me . . . Between the salt waters and sands of the sea') are impossible, since they are symbolic of youth's aspiration towards the impossible. Why the strange title of the song? I think that it signifies that life is organic, that land and its flower, the rose, take on human qualities, just as man must adapt to the land and the sea and the inhuman to survive. Categories are mixed; roses grow merry; certainly 'in time', which carries the two meanings of 'eventually and 'in rhythm', refers forward to Finn's gaining the heart of the circle and putting his own life in harmony.

He goes home, and, uncertain yet about Una, seeks the House of Peace. (He has, of course, made his peace with Catrine and Roddie with his presents to their child.) For the first time the House of Peace gives him no comfort, yet this is appropriate, since through unease he is driven to the Birch Wood and Una. The House has not failed him. Thus the last chapter is self-explanatory. Finn is at the heart of the circle, literally, as he waits for the wedding rituals in the centre of the stones. He has his new 34-foot boat, *Gannet*, his new wife, his new relationship with his mother and Roddie, and his new maturity. He has come full circle to where his father was twenty years before. The 'other landscape' is here too — for Finn has at last completed a circle of wisdom around himself.

6 Gunn and Gibbon

From the achievement of the Scottish Renaissance Neil Gunn emerges as the novelist of regeneration and hope, while Gibbon seems finally to speak of despair. They are the Light and the Dark, the positive and negative of the spectrum of the attitudes of the Renaissance writers.

However, the parallels remain, almost over-riding the authors' differences. Broadly, these come down to ten major points.

Both use the Golden Age myth: that belief that Man before institutionalisation and so-called 'civilisation' was not primitive man, and that the main events of Scottish history, from the Reformation in 1560 to the Industrial Revolution and the Highland Clearances corrupted a communal innocence. The *art* of both is based upon such a belief. Consequently, both employ the same device whereby ancient time past is contrasted and juxtaposed with time present through the use of 'Great Memory' or Jung's notion of 'the collective unconscious'. Central characters move suddenly back in their time-awareness to their ancestral past — although both allow this use of what is in one interpretation a supernatural experience and in another rational explanation.

They share a resentment of the workings of 'Authority', of British Imperialism. Gunn, however, understates his case, to my mind making it more forcibly, while Gibbon becomes sometimes hysterical. Both *The Silver Darlings* and *A Scots Quair* have as central theme the callous destruction of a good local community life by a remote power system. They each are deeply aware in their own environment of racial traditions which make up modern Scotland. Gunn contrasts Tormad, the Pict unused to the sea, with Roddie, the Viking in his element; and similarly Chris and Long Rob are of Venriconian Pict stock (Rob with a Viking element), while Ewan Tavendale represents a Celtic and Highland volatility.

They share techniques and methods. There is uncanny similarity in the way *Sunset Song* and *The Silver Darlings* make the Standing Stones and the House of Peace respectively play almost exactly the same roles, acting as a sort of symbolic 'backbone' in each novel. Both use the same method to show social and personal dehumanisation, by presenting 'ghosts' — that is, characters who have become shells of their former selves, like Ronnie in *The Silver Darlings*, Ewan and Chae in *Sunset Song*; and the same symbolism is employed for the agencies which work this change, such as the tall ship which destroys Tormad in Gunn, and the machines and motors of Gibbon in *A Scots Quair*; these are the portents of tragedy.

The major fiction of each is allegory for the Scottish situation. Finn represents Finn MacCoul, ancient Celtic leader and hero, personifying Scotland reviving from Culloden, Clearance and wasteland, Chris Guthrie is 'Chris Caledonia', the nation of Scotland and its soul, moving through its peasant, rural and city stages. In presenting their allegories each writer resorted to similar techniques of language. Faced with the problem of speaking for a region with an inaccessible dialect or language, Gibbon invented 'the speak', capturing not so much the exact words of his people as their rhythms and their syntax. Gunn likewise found the rhythms and 'feel' of Gaelic in English.

Finally, in the presentation of a wasteland, spiritual as well as physical, both create in their major work a relationship between a woman and her male child. Male leadership is shown lacking; from the mother woman, who represents the land, the male child is shown as taking on his role as New Man, saviour of his community.

Again, one sees the profound differences. Gunn shows life coming from death: Catrine of *The Silver Darlings* gives Finn as symbol of hope to the folk, whereas Chris ultimately retreats from her son's values and hope. And Ewan's vision of the folk, of human nature, is fundamentally pessimistic, since humanity requires in his view to be led. Finn on the other hand, sees that his own self and life are paramount, and becomes important to the community through legend and example.

Both writers are poets, magnificent users of tradition and symbol. In the work of modern Scottish writers like George Mackay Brown of Orkney, Iain Crichton Smith from the Western Isles, William McIlvanney, Archie Hind, Alan Sharp, from the cities, the love of 'The Dear Green Place', the dream of a fundamental Scottish and rural goodness deep down, is abundantly evidenced — witness the recurrence of the image and word 'green' in titles of modern Scottish fiction and poetry. The achievement of Gunn and Gibbon, however, although continually regenerating modern Scottish writing, has never been excelled.

Bibliography

List of Works by Neil Gunn

(Publishers of texts in print at the time of writing this book listed after original date of publication.)

The Grey Coast   London, 1926 (revised ed. Porpoise Press 1931) (Souvenir).

Hidden Doors   Edinburgh, 1929.

Morning Tide   Edinburgh, 1931 (Souvenir).

Back Home   (One-act-play), Glasgow, 1932.

The Lost Glen   Edinburgh, 1932 (First published Scots Mag. 1929).

Sun Circle   Edinburgh, 1933.

Butcher's Broom   Edinburgh, 1934 (Souvenir).

Whisky and Scotland: A Practical and Spiritual Survey   London, 1935 (Souvenir).

Highland River   Edinburgh, 1937.

Choosing a Play: A Comedy of Community Drama   Edinburgh, 1938.

Off in a Boat   London, 1938.

Old Music   (one-act-play), London, 1939.

Net Results   (one-act-play), London, 1939.

Wild Geese Overhead   London, 1939.

Second Sight   London, 1940.

The Silver Darlings   London, 1941 (Faber).

Young Art and Old Hector   London, 1942 (Souvenir).

Storm and Precipice and Other Pieces   (anthology of Gunn's writing) London, 1942.

The Serpent   London, 1943 (Souvenir).

The Green Isle of the Great Deep   London, 1944 (Souvenir).

The Key of the Chest   London, 1945 (Portway Reprints, Cedric Chivers, Bath).

The Drinking Well   London, 1946 (Souvenir).

The Shadow   London, 1948.
The Silver Bough   London, 1948.
The Lost Chart   London, 1949.
Highland Pack   London, 1949.
The White Hour   London, 1950.
The Well at the World's End   London, 1951 (Portway Reprints).
Bloodhunt   London, 1952.
The Other Landscape   London, 1954.
The Atom of Delight   London, 1956.

List of Works by Lewis Grassic Gibbon (Leslie Mitchell)

Hanno: or the Future of Exploration   London, 1928 (Mitchell).
Stained Radiance   London, 1930 (Mitchell).
The Thirteenth Disciple   London, 1931 (Paul Harris, Edinburgh) (Mitchell).
The Calends of Cairo   London, 1931 (Mitchell).
Three Go Back   London, 1932 (Mitchell).
The Lost Trumpet   London, 1932 (Mitchell).
Sunset Song   London, 1932 (Hutchinson, Pan, Longman) (Gibbon).
Persian Dawns, Egyptian Nights   London, 1932 (Mitchell).
Image and Superscription   London, 1933 (Mitchell).
Cloud Howe   London, 1933 (Hutchinson, Pan) (Gibbon).
Spartacus   London, 1933 (Hutchinson) (Mitchell).
Niger: The Life of Mungo Park   Edinburgh, 1934 (Gibbon).
The Conquest of the Maya   London, 1934 (Mitchell).
Gay Hunter   London, 1934 (Mitchell).
Scottish Scene: or the Intelligent Man's Guide to Albyn   London, 1934 (Gibbon, in collaboration with Hugh MacDiarmid)
Grey Granite   London, 1934 (Hutchinson, Pan) (Gibbon).
Nine Against the Unknown   London, 1934 (Mitchell *and* Gibbon).
A Scots Hairst   London, 1967 (Gibbon essays, Scottish short stories, a selection of Mitchell school work and later stories and poems by Ian Munro).
Smeddum: Stories and Essays   London, 1980 (Five Scottish stories and four essays of Gibbon, edited by D. M. Budge).

The Speak of the Mearns   Edinburgh, 1982 (an unfinished novella edited by Ian Campbell).

Recommended Reading

General

Blake, George   *Barrie and the Kailyard School*, London, 1951.
   Useful introduction to the Scottish fiction Gibbon and Gunn disliked!

Bruce, George and Munro, Ian   *Two Essays*, Edinburgh, 1971.
   Short introduction to Gunn and Gibbon from National Library of Scotland.

Campbell, Ian (ed)   *Essays in Nineteenth-Century Scottish Fiction*, Edinburgh, 1980.

Campbell, Ian *Kailyard: a New Assessment*, Ramsay Head Press, Edinburgh, 1981.

Craig, David   *Scottish Literature and the Scottish People*, London, 1961.

Glen, Duncan   *Hugh MacDiarmid and the Scottish Renaissance*, Edinburgh and London, 1964.

Hart, Francis   *The Scottish Novel*, London. 1978.
   Hart's work on Scottish fiction is the starting point for the serious student; especially good on Gunn.

Lindsay, Maurice   *History of Scottish Literature*, London, 1977.

Wittig, Kurt   *The Scottish Tradition in Literature*, Edinburgh, 1958.
   Sees Gunn as the highpoint of the Scottish renaissance.

Gunn

See especially the work of *Francis Hart* below.

Gibbon, Lewis Grassic   'Literature Lights' in *Scottish Scene*, and *A Scots Hairst*.

Gifford, Douglas   'Neil M. Gunn's Fiction of Delight' in *Scottish International Review* May 1972.

Grieve, C. M.   (Hugh MacDiarmid)   'Neil M. Gunn' in Chapter 33, *Contemporary Scottish Studies*, London, 1926.

Hart, Francis   'The Hunter and the Circle: Neil Gunn's Fiction of Violence' in *Studies in Scottish Literature*, Vol. I, 1963–4.

Hart, Francis, and Pick, John   *Neil M. Gunn: A Highland Life*, London, 1981. Essential new information on Gunn.

Morrison, David (ed)   *Essays on Neil M. Gunn*, Thurso, 1971.
Five authoritative essays including Hart 'Beyond History and Tragedy: Neil Gunn's Fiction of Violence.'

Scott, Alexander and Gifford, Douglas (eds)   *Neil M. Gunn: the Man and the Writer*, Edinburgh, 1973.
Twenty essays covering biography, fiction, short stories, bibliography, including Hart 'Neil M. Gunn: A Brief Memoir' and 'Comedy and Transcendence in Gunn's Later Fiction'.

Gibbon

Budge, D. M.   Commentary/Introduction to *Smeddum: Stories and Essays*, London 1980. (Longman *Heritage of Literature* series)

Caird, J. B.   'Lewis Grassic Gibbon and his Contribution to the Scottish Novel' in *Essays in Literature*, Edinburgh, 1936.

Gunn, Neil M.   'Tradition and Magic in the Work of Lewis Grassic Gibbon' in *The Scots Magazine*, 1938.

Low, John T.   Commentary/Afterword to his edition of *Sunset Song*, London, 1971. (Longman *Heritage of Literature* series) The best edition.

Munro, Ian S.   *Leslie Mitchell: Lewis Grassic Gibbon*, Edinburgh and London, 1966.
The only biography.

Wagner, Geoffrey   'The Greatest Since Galt' in *Essays in Criticism*, Vol. 2, 1952.

Wagner, Geoffrey   'James Leslie Mitchell/Lewis Grassic Gibbon: A Chronological Checklist' in *The Bibliotheck*, Vol. I, 1956.

Wilson, P. Joyce   'Freedom and God: some implications of the key speech in *A Scots Quair*', in *Scottish Literary Journal*, 1980.

Young, Douglas   *Beyond the Sunset*, Aberdeen, 1973.
The best critical work.